FACEBOOK® MARKETING

Leveraging Facebook's Features for Your Marketing Campaigns

THIRD EDITION

BRIAN CARTER
JUSTIN LEVY

800 East 96th Street
Indianapolis, Indiana 46240 USA

~cebook Marketing: Leveraging ~acebook's Features for Your Marketing Campaigns

Copyright © 2012 by Que Publishing

ISBN-13: 978-0-7897-4113-4
ISBN-10: 0-7897-4113-X

Library of Congress Cataloging-in-Publication Data is on file.

Printed in the United States of America

First Printing: December 2012

Trademarks

All terms mentioned in this book that are known to be trademarks or service marks have been appropriately capitalized. Que Publishing cannot attest to the accuracy of this information. Use of a term in this book should not be regarded as affecting the validity of any trademark or service mark.

Warning and Disclaimer

Every effort has been made to make this book as complete and as accurate as possible, but no warranty or fitness is implied. The information provided is on an "as is" basis. The authors and the publisher shall have neither liability nor responsibility to any person or entity with respect to any loss or damages arising from the information contained in this book or from the use of programs accompanying it.

Bulk Sales

Que Publishing offers excellent discounts on this book when ordered in quantity for bulk purchases or special sales. For more information, please contact

U.S. Corporate and Government Sales
1-800-382-3419
corpsales@pearsontechgroup.com

For sales outside of the U.S., please contact

International Sales
international@pearson.com

CONTENTS AT A GLANCE

TABLE OF CONTENTS

About the Authors

Brian Carter is respected as one of the elite Internet marketing experts in the world. His hands-on business experience, cutting edge insights, background in improv and stand-up comedy culminate in a speaker and trainer who leaves every audience not only entertained, but armed with powerful strategies and tactics.

Brian has 12 years experience with Google, Twitter, and Facebook marketing, both as a consultant and marketing agency director. He has trained and managed Gen X and Gen Y employees, in addition to the more than 5,000 students of his FanReach Facebook marketing online course. He is a social media keynote speaker who combines entertainment, comedy, and education into hilarious event experiences.

Brian develops strategies and builds search visibility and social marketing fanbases for companies of all sizes, including well-known entities such as Universal Studios, the U.S. Army, Hardee's, and Carl's Jr. He is quoted in the book *Twitter Marketing for Dummies* and has been quoted and profiled by *Information Week*, *U.S. News & World Report*, *The Wall Street Journal*, and *Entrepreneur Magazine*.

Brian writes for two of the most popular marketing blogs, Search Engine Journal and AllFacebook, and his combined readership exceeds 100,000 people. He has more than 30,000 Twitter followers and an overall reach of more than 50,000 fans through Facebook, LinkedIn, and his other marketing channels. A speaker and trainer for top marketing conferences that include Socialize, SEOmoz, SMX, Pubcon, and the American Marketing Association, Brian is one of the nation's leading experts in Internet marketing.

Justin Levy is the head of social communications for the Online Services Division of Citrix Systems, where he serves as editor-in-chief of Workshifting.com, a blog dedicated to the mobile and diversified workforce and ranked as one of the top 1% blogs worldwide according to Alexa. When not managing the blog, Justin focuses on influencer relations, developing thought leadership and supporting internal teams.

Prior to joining Citrix, Justin was an Executive Director at New Marketing Labs, a social media and digital communications agency. While at New Marketing Labs, Justin worked with clients ranging from Fortune 500 brands such as SAS, Sony, PepsiCo, and Microsoft. Justin also served as Co-Chair and Conference Director of the Inbound Marketing Summit.

Justin is a partner at Caminito Argentinean Steakhouse, ranked for two years in a row as the #1 steakhouse in western Massachusetts. Through the use of social media marketing techniques, Justin successfully grew the steakhouse at least 20% in sales for 30+ months straight. As part of this, Justin is a cofounder of primecutsblog.com, a blog focusing on teaching readers cooking techniques, tips, and recipes. Because of this success, Justin and Caminito have been featured in multiple business and marketing books and have been profiled by some of the most successful marketing blogs and mainstream publications.

Justin writes and creates media of all kinds over at justinrlevy.com. Justin is a sought-after public speaker on the topics of social media, marketing, and technology and has been interviewed by mainstream media sources including FOX Business, Associated Press, *Inc. Magazine*, and the *Boston Globe*.

Justin is the author of the second edition of this book, *Facebook Marketing: Designing Your Next Marketing Campaign.*

Dedication

I'd like to dedicate this book to my parents and my wife, who've made me a much better person than I would have been otherwise.
—**Brian Carter**

This book is dedicated to everyone who has supported, motivated, and encouraged me over the years. Thank you for always believing in me.
—**Justin Levy**

Acknowledgments

Thanks to Katherine Bull and the Pearson Education team, including Romny French, Anne Goebel, and Brandon Prebynski, who made this third edition possible.

We Want to Hear from You!

As the reader of this book, *you* are our most important critic and commentator. We value your opinion and want to know what we're doing right, what we could do better, what areas you'd like to see us publish in, and any other words of wisdom you're willing to pass our way.

As the Editor-in-Chief for Que Publishing, I welcome your comments. You can email or write me directly to let me know what you did or didn't like about this book—as well as what we can do to make our books better.

Please note that I cannot help you with technical problems related to the topic of this book. We do have a User Services group, however, where I will forward specific technical questions related to the book.

When you write, please be sure to include this book's title and author as well as your name, email address, and phone number. I will carefully review your comments and share them with the author and editors who worked on the book.

Email: feedback@quepublishing.com

Mail: Greg Wiegand
         Editor-in-Chief
         Que Publishing
         800 East 96th Street
         Indianapolis, IN 46240 USA

Reader Services

Visit our website and register this book at quepublishing.com/register for convenient access to any updates, downloads, or errata that might be available for this book.

Introduction

From Dorm Room to Board Room: The Growth of Social Networks

Over the past several years, social networks have become increasingly popular as they made their way into mainstream society, mainly because users have the ability to communicate in both real-time and asynchronously with a wide group of people. It is important to remember that the ability to use the Internet to communicate with a diverse and worldwide audience is not new and cannot be attributed solely to tools such as MySpace, Facebook, and Twitter. Connecting instantaneously with people from all around the world has been available to us since Prodigy decided to allow people to set up user groups around topics that interested them.

This paved the way to the creation of forum boards, user groups, chat rooms, IRC, instant messaging, and eventually, social networks as we know them today.

Today, these social networks come in different shapes, sizes, and specialties.

- Do you love taking photos? Hop on Flickr.
- Want to communicate in short bursts of messages in real-time? Head over to Twitter.
- A sucker for video? There's a service a few people have heard of called YouTube.
- Want something a little more specialized? There are almost one billion different niche social networks to choose from on Ning.

You see, there is a social network for just about every broad and specific subject you could possibly want. Some are more mainstream and "sticky" than others; therefore, there's more engagement and sharing by the community, and more iterating of the platform by the founding company.

These tools enable a single person to develop a personal brand or small business brand that can compete with household consumer brands. The development of these personal brands, social networks, and blogs enables people to now be in control of *what* news others see. These social networks allow for the management of your online reputation. Besides these benefits, they create the ability for one person to use a platform to talk to thousands of people simply by pressing the Enter key. Social networks enable regular, normal, run-of-the-mill individuals to become influencers and trusted resources to their communities. Yes, now *you* can develop your own personal communities. These communities can have a direct impact on your ability to build your business successfully by interacting with your prospects and customers online and building a strong fan base.

Social networks and blogs allow a wine store owner to connect with his community and help to grow his business from $4 million per year to over $60 million per year in revenue. These tools have helped a guy from north of Boston to develop such a strong community that they helped catapult a book he wrote onto the *New York Times* bestsellers list only two days after the book was on store shelves. But, these tools have not only been beneficial to individuals. They have also helped some of the largest companies in the world reach out and start connecting with their customers on a one-to-one basis.

Businesses have greatly benefited from turning to social networks and integrating them as part of their marketing, communications, and customer service strategies.

Using social networks has allowed businesses that embrace these tools to "humanize themselves." What do we mean by the term *humanize*?

For decades, companies have continued to grow through their ability to properly manage their brand by successfully marketing logos, catch phrases, slogans, and tag lines, all of which help to develop brand recognition. These companies became known by our ability to recognize their logos and get their jingles stuck in our heads, or know the catchy tag line at the end of every commercial. At the same time, these same companies, in an effort to improve their bottom line, routinely looked at implementing systems and processes that automated as much as possible. Need to talk to customer service? Sure, there is a number to call. But, first, you're going to have to hit 1. Then 2. Type your account number. Type it again because you screwed up the first time. Say your last name. Now you're finally transferred to a human but because you hit 2 instead of 3 during the second step, you were sent to the wrong department. Now you have to be transferred elsewhere, where you have to repeat all the information that you just inputted.

It's barriers like these that, while beneficial to the corporation, prevent them from highlighting the humans and personalities that help the corporation to function on a daily basis. Social networks help to change this. Humans can showcase the individual personalities that help make them who they are. Companies can now cut out the phone trees and instantaneously interact with a single customer who is having an issue, which, to the customer, is one of the most serious things going on in his life at the very moment.

Besides just being active on social networks, these tools also enable businesses to, as Chris Brogan describes it, "grow bigger ears." You see, at any given moment, there are multiple conversations taking place about you, your brand, your products or services, your competition, and your industry. Imagine if you could monitor all this chatter in real time and had the ability to quickly respond? That would be valuable to you as a business, right? Hint: You want to be nodding your head up and down as fast as possible. If you're not, then put this book down, run headfirst into the wall, and start over again.

By way of the amount of data that users pour into these social networks on a daily basis, they allow us to monitor all those conversations with listening tools. These listening tools can alert us to any mentions of anything that is of interest to us. Someone bashes you on a blog post? The software service your company sells crashes for a user during a big presentation, so he complains online? Your competition announces a major restructuring, product, or financial news? Yep, all these situations and much more can be monitored. In fact, these tools, because of their real-time nature, routinely provide information faster than Google can index it and quicker than news organizations can mobilize to broadcast.

Social networks have helped to grow businesses, elevate normal people to web celebrities, bring celebrities down to a human level, launch music careers, change national sentiment toward entire industries, and assist in building and growing a community so strong that it helped to elect the 44th President of the United States of America.

One of the fastest growing and most popular social networks ever to be launched is Facebook. With nearly 800 million users who generate billions of pieces of content, the social network has a larger population than most countries. When you first join Facebook, you immediately understand how it can be used to connect with family and friends. However, many people find themselves questioning the viability of using Facebook as a main form of communication professionally. Companies, rightfully so, have many questions regarding security, privacy, and how a website where you can comment on what your friends are doing, upload pictures, videos, and become a fan of just about anything in the world can actually help them to move needles that are important to them.

Throughout this book, we will tackle these very issues and help show you, both strategically and tactically, how Facebook can be used within your business. But first, let's start by exploring how a little social network that was created in a dorm room has become the behemoth that it is today.

About Mark Zuckerberg

Mark Zuckerberg (shown in Figure 0.1) was born on May 14, 1984 and was raised in Dobbs Ferry, NY. Although it would be a few years before Zuckerberg would create the top social network in the world, he began coding at an early age, while he was in middle school. Zuckerberg attended Phillips Exeter Academy, where he devised Synapse, a music player that leveraged artificial intelligence to learn users' listening habits. The technology that Zuckerberg created was so intriguing that it brought both Microsoft and AOL calling; both corporations tried recruiting Zuckerberg before he decided to attend Harvard University. But that was not the only project keeping Zuckerberg busy while he attended Phillips Exeter Academy. Zuckerberg also built a version of the popular game, Risk, in addition to a program to help improve communications within his father's office. After Phillips Exeter Academy, Zuckerberg moved on to Harvard where he studied computer science.

Figure 0.1   *Mark Zuckerberg, Cofounder, CEO, and President of Facebook.*

The Early Days

What would become the world's most popular social network all started in February 2004, when Mark Zuckerberg launched The Facebook, originally located at thefacebook.com (see Figure 0.2). Although he later became the richest person in the world under 25, Mark Zuckerberg was just a sophomore at Harvard University when he developed The Facebook.

The Facebook was a follow-up to Zuckerberg's Harvard version of a popular rating website, HOT or NOT. Zuckerberg called it Facemash, and it was intended to allow students at Harvard University to compare other students based on their online dorm Facebooks.

HOT or NOT, as shown in Figure 0.3, was a popular rating site, founded in October 2000 by James Hong and Jim Young, that allowed users to vote whether pictures of people that were submitted to the site were HOT or NOT. As the HOT or NOT website describes:

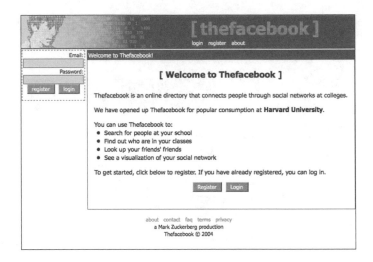

Figure 0.2   *The original login screen to TheFacebook.com that launched on February 4, 2004, for Harvard University students only.*

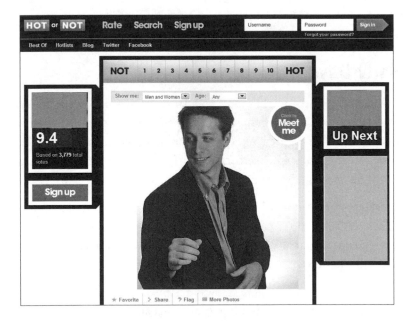

Figure 0.3   *One of the original landing pages for HOTorNOT.com, which, at the height of its growth, would bring in annual revenues of approximately $5 million.*

HOT or NOT is the original place to rate, date, and hook up with
single people 18–34. With millions rated using HOT or NOT's proprietary "RATE" feature, HOT or NOT is the official home of hot-
ness...users can "MEET" other members through HOT or NOT's
exclusive DoubleMatch™ dating engine. HOT or NOT also offers
other fun options such as real-time chat, virtual flowers and gifts, and
HOTLists™, which let members share their passions through personal
selections of over 220,000 pictures of bands, movies, sports, TV shows,
products, and hobbies.

At its height, HOT or NOT raked in an annual revenue approximated at $5 million
with net profits of $2 million. Whether, at the time, HOT or NOT had already hit
this success, and if it had, if Zuckerberg had known about it, the service was still
very popular among college students. Therefore, it is no surprise that Zuckerberg
saw an opportunity to create a private, internal network similar to the popular rating service, reserved only for Harvard students. Also, the basic tenets of the service
aren't features that would be hard for someone who had been coding his entire life
to create.

The Facemash site launched on October 28, 2003 but was shut down by Harvard
administration officials only a few days later because, to gain access to the pictures,
Zuckerberg had hacked Harvard's computer network and copied over each of
the nine residential houses' databases of ID photos.[1] So, how did a HOT or NOT
knockoff eventually iterate to become the world's largest and most popular social
network to date?

The Teenage Years

The Facebook was launched and, at first, was available only to Harvard University students. In March 2004, only one month after its initial launch, Zuckerberg
expanded access to Stanford, Yale, and Columbia. Then Zuckerberg quickly
expanded access to all Ivy League universities, then to Boston area universities
and colleges, and then across the United States and Canada. Although nothing
specifically points to the geographic location of Harvard University as one of the
reasons for the early explosive growth, it could be argued that it had a big effect.

In the greater Boston area, there are well over 100 colleges and universities. The Northeast has the largest concentration of colleges and universities in the country. This helped Zuckerberg spread the social network quickly as it created demand for access as friends from different schools chatted with one another.

During its initial growth spurt at Harvard, Zuckerberg brought on Eduardo Saverin, Dustin Moskovitz, Andrew McCollum, and Chris Hughes to help with programming, graphic design, promotion, and other related tasks. The Facebook would later incorporate as a business during the summer of 2004. In June 2004, only four months after the platform's inception, Facebook would receive its first investment totaling $500,000 from Peter Thiel, cofounder of PayPal. For The Facebook to continue its Cinderella story, it would be necessary for the company to be located at the epicenter of technology, Silicon Valley. The Facebook moved operations out of the dorm rooms at Harvard and out to Palo Alto, California.

In 2005, The Facebook purchased facebook.com for $200,000 and dropped "The" from its name. Later that year, in September 2005, approximately a year and one-half after the initial launch, Facebook opened its network to high schools. It would be another year, in September 2006, before Facebook would completely open the network to anyone older than 13 with a valid email address.[2]

During this time, Facebook continued to receive injections of cash to help it scale its operations to accommodate for the increase in demand from its users. In 2005, Facebook received venture capital funding from Accel Partners to the tune of $12.7 million.[3] Facebook would receive another injection from Greylock Partners totaling $27.5 million in 2006.[4]

To help Facebook continue expanding into international markets, in October 2007, Facebook and Microsoft expanded an advertising deal that gave Microsoft a $240 million equity stake in the social network.[5] As a main pillar of Facebook's current revenue model, Facebook launched Facebook Ads a month later, in November 2007.[6]

Coming into Adulthood

In January 2010, Mark Zuckerberg announced that Facebook had signed on its 400 millionth user. Consider that in September 2009, Zuckerberg announced the 300 millionth user, and not too long before that, in July 2009, he announced via the Facebook Blog that the network had surpassed its 250 millionth user since the site launched in February 2004. In only approximately two months, the social network had signed up an additional 50 million users. To put that number into perspective, consider that in April 2009, Zuckerberg had announced that Facebook had passed the 200 millionth user mark. The growth from 200 to 250 million users took Facebook approximately 90 days. The growth from 250 to 300 million users took roughly 60 days. That is a growth rate of approximately 833,000 users every day, which translates to approximately 35,000 users per hour, or 578 every minute. Some estimates place the growth rate at approximately 750,000 new users per day.

Each time Facebook hit another growth milestone, it did it in record timing compared to previous accomplishments. Think Facebook is going away anytime soon? Consider the following chronological growth patterns (see Figure 0.4):

- February 2004: Facebook launches.
- December 2004: Facebook reaches **1 million** active users.
- December 2005: Facebook reaches **5.5 million** active users.
- December 2006: Facebook reaches **12 million** active users.
- April 2007: Facebook reaches **20 million** active users.
- October 2007: Facebook reaches **50 million** active users.
- August 2008: Facebook reaches **100 million** active users.
- January 2009: Facebook reaches **150 million** active users.
- February 2009: Facebook reaches **175 million** active users.
- April 2009: Facebook reaches **200 million** active users.
- July 2009: Facebook reaches **250 million** active users.
- September 2009: Facebook reaches **300 million** active users.
- February 2010: Facebook reaches **450 million** users.
- June 2011: Facebook reaches **750 million** users.

From 2008 to June 2009, Facebook grew 157 percent, gaining an estimated 208 million visitors. As of June 2009, Facebook was receiving approximately 340 million unique visitors per month, making it the fourth largest website in the world. The only websites with more monthly traffic are Google, Microsoft, and Yahoo!. During the month of June 2009, it is estimated that Facebook grew by 24 million unique visitors as compared to May 2009. This type of traffic, and the growing importance within the fabric of the interwebs, has led Facebook, according to paidContent.org, to pass Google as the top traffic driver to large sites.

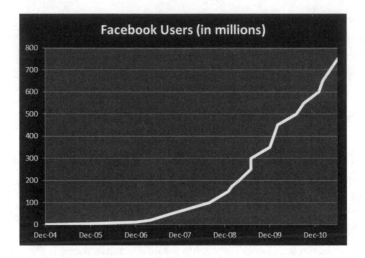

Figure 0.4   *The rapid growth of Facebook's user base.*

To comprehend such astronomical numbers, let's look at Facebook at the 200 million active users mark. When Facebook hit the 200 million active users milestone, it produced a video about the race to 200 million people and provided these comparisons:

- It took 20,000 years for the world population to reach 200 million.
- It would take 46.5 years for 200 million babies to be born in the United States.
- If Facebook were a country, it would be the world's fifth most populous country, bigger than Brazil, Russia, and Japan.

When you hear such large numbers of users flocking to any service, it always raises the question: Are they actually using the service or are they just signing up for an account that remains dormant?

For Facebook, its users are actively participating in the conversations and are spending a lot of their time doing so. Facebook publishes the following stats on its website:[7]

- More than 700 billion minutes are spent on Facebook each day (worldwide).
- More than 800 million active users has returned to the site in the past 30 days.
- More 50% of active users log in to Facebook on any given day.

- The average user has 130 friends.

- The average user is connected to 80 pages, groups, and events.

- The average user creates 90 pieces of content each month.

- More than 2 billion posts are liked and commented on per day.

- More than 250 million photos are uploaded each day.

- More than 70 translations are available on the site.

- About 75% of Facebook users are outside the United States.

- People on Facebook install 20 million applications every day.

- Every month, more than 500 million people engage with Facebook on external websites.

- More than 2.5 million websites have integrated with Facebook, including more than 80 of comScore's U.S. Top 100 websites and more than half of comScore's Global Top 100 websites. More than 7 million apps and websites have integrated with Facebook.

- More than 350 million active users currently access Facebook through their mobile devices.

- People who use Facebook on their mobile devices are twice as active on Facebook than nonmobile users.

Facebook is on pace to sign 1 billion active users by the start of 2012.

So why is everyone running to join Facebook? Facebook seemed to come of age at a time when simple and functional design wins out. Over the years, Facebook has continued to maintain a clean, organized user interface, despite adding tons of new features. Facebook is similar to Google in that way. Besides being a superior search engine compared to Yahoo!, MSN, and others, Google wins over users because it is simple and easy to use, yet is a powerful engine. Facebook represents the same for the social networking space.

Facebook provides an easy-to-understand interface, thus making it appeal to all ages. For the less tech-savvy, it is manageable without a lot of help. Those who are tech-savvy can take full advantage of the multitude of settings, options, and flexibility of the platform to share and engage.

In 2010 and 2011, Facebook came to better reflect all age groups. Half of Facebook is age 25 to 64; the 35–44 age group represents one-sixth of Facebook's population, and the 45–54 group is one-eighth. SocialBakers.com, a Facebook statistics website, estimates that 64% of Americans who use the Internet are Facebook users.

Facebook is no longer only for college students. Facebook is now for your parents and your grandparents. It is for your colleagues and your supervisors. It's for individuals, celebrities, brands, products, services, musicians, and anyone else who finds it useful to fish where the fish are, whether it's for friends, ex-lovers, business opportunities, fans, or constituents. Facebook is now mainstream and poised to continue its rapid growth rate.

To highlight Facebook's injection into the mainstream, in January 2009—during the inauguration of the 44th President of the United States, Barack Obama—CNN Live and Facebook teamed up to provide real-time updates from Facebook's users in line with the live coverage by CNN. The result was a live video stream window side-by-side with a Facebook integration that displayed status updates, as shown in Figure 0.5, from all Facebook users regarding the inauguration. It is estimated that 8,500 status updates per minute were captured during the inauguration. After the massive success of this integration, Facebook would again make a similar partnership, but this time with the NBA. During the NBA All-Star game, Facebook provided a real-time stream of status updates about the 2009 NBA All-Star game. Facebook followed this with a live stream integration during the 2009 Grammys.

Figure 0.5   *During President Obama's inauguration speech, Facebook logged 8,500 status updates per minute. (Screenshot by David Orban.)*

Such partnerships have proven successful for Facebook as it serves as a proving ground to those who are resistant to using the service. Certainly, there were probably viewers of CNN Live, the Grammys, and the NBA All-Star game who are skeptical about the service or continued to think it was only for high school and college students. But having the integration in place with a network such as CNN, which is arguably the top news network, during one of the most important chapters of our nation's history to date, served as a milestone for the social network.

Facebook isn't only growing its user base at a blistering pace, it continues to build out its organization and gain market power. To accommodate this growth, during 2009, Facebook opened its new headquarters located in Palo Alto. During 2010, Facebook grew its internal team by adding a new office in Austin, Texas, with an initial group of 300 team members. That is in addition to other smaller, satellite offices all over the country. No longer is Facebook working out of multiple rented office spaces, coffee shops, and bookstores.

With the rapid growth and popularity that Facebook continues to experience, there have been several estimated valuations of the company. Probably the best stat to look at is from a May 2009 investment from Digital Sky Technologies to the tune of $200 million. The investment deal between Digital Sky Technologies and Facebook was for preferred stock at a $10 billion valuation. With this intensive growth has also come fame and fortune for its founder, Mark Zuckerberg.

Zuckerberg is the youngest person to ever be named to the Forbes 400 list. In 2008, Forbes estimated Zuckerberg's net worth at approximately $1.5 billion, making him the 321st richest person in the United States. In 2010 he was named *Time*'s Person of the Year, and in 2011 his personal wealth is estimated to be $13.5 billion. He is now the 19th richest person in the United States and is 52nd among billionaires worldwide.

Although Facebook has faced competition from other social networks such as Twitter, FriendFeed, MySpace, Flickr, and other smaller services, it seems as though it can't be stopped. In August 2009, Facebook acquired FriendFeed for roughly $50 million. This purchase came after approximately one year of FriendFeed continuing to grow its user base and implementing new features that left Facebook users begging for them. As these new features were released, interestingly enough, they would appear on the Facebook platform not long after.

This is one of the marks of Facebook so far. When other services implement features that its platform currently does not support, usually, not too long afterward, we see the same services appear in Facebook. Most notably was the integration in February 2009, before its acquisition of FriendFeed, of the Likes feature that had become so popular among FriendFeed users. In September 2009, Facebook responded to demands from the users to implement a status-tagging feature to notify other users or Pages when they've been mentioned in a status update. Again, similar to the Likes feature from FriendFeed, this alert feature is a combination of @ replies in Twitter coupled with the tagging feature in Facebook Photos and Videos. In 2011, Facebook teamed up with Skype and Microsoft, and Facebook functionality has been added inside of Skype. There is now a real Microsoft/Facebook alliance that threatens Google's Internet dominance.

Justin opened his Facebook account after he graduated from college, although only by a couple months; he was not part of the initial surge of people who rushed to the service. Although it is interesting to see the fast growth of the 35+ group (which now composes two-thirds of all Facebook users), he has spoken with many people who have told him stories about multiple generations of their families being on Facebook. He doesn't foresee his grandparents jumping on the service any-time soon (and in fact, Brian's mom refuses to join, and his 99-year-old grandma doesn't even like the telephone) but Justin thinks it would be interesting to receive a comment from them to a status or link he posted.

We know what you're thinking. First, you probably didn't realize that Facebook was that large. Don't worry—you're not alone. A number of people are still reluc-tant to believe it. But, now that you know, how can you jump in and get involved (or more involved)? Can you take the available features and turn Facebook into a successful tool for communicating with your prospects and customers? And what about privacy?

All these questions and plenty more will be answered in the upcoming chapters. Along the way we explain the features and their basic functions, and then highlight how you can begin using them for your business. For those of you who like case studies and stories of success, we have you covered. If you walk about after finish-ing this book and think, "Oh, that was interesting," and never do anything with the information, then I failed to do my job. If, instead, you take this book, scribble throughout it, call a team meeting, grab a blank whiteboard, and start strategizing about how you're going to integrate Facebook (and other social networks) into the fold of your business, fantastic.

The most important thing is for you to keep an open mind as you flip the pages of this book. Understand that the social networks, especially ones such as Facebook, *are* the new way to communicate and market your brand. You can either choose to embrace it or watch your competition pass you as they figure it out. For the nonbe-lievers who are reading this book, this is your call to action. Enough is enough. It's time to accept that social networks aren't going anywhere. For those of you who are already deeply engaged in social networks such as Facebook, we hope we can shed light on some ideas and features that you haven't previously considered using.

A preview of the book:

This book is a deep dive into how Facebook can be leveraged by your company starting today. This book is not just a "Facebook is cool and you should join" type of book. This book provides you with actionable information that you can begin implementing into your business as you read each chapter. It gives you the ammunition you need to convince your boss, your board, your IT team, or your employees why they should be investing time and money in "just another social network." This book also shows you HOW to implement the various features of Facebook for your business. You can use this book as a step-by-step guide, keeping it right beside your keyboard, as you start to build Pages, launch ad campaigns, set up Groups, and explore Places and the number of other features applicable for your business.

This book addresses these concepts. We start with a very brief overview of Facebook's history and the basics of getting around the site. We then dig deep into the major Facebook business features, including Facebook Pages, Groups, Ads, Apps, Places, Deals, and Facebook Connect. We'll discuss privacy and options that protect your business. Then we explore some of those companies that have used Facebook to the utmost to reach their business goals. You'll be able to extrapolate some of the concepts that they use, break them down, and discover what will most help *your* company. This book finishes with where Facebook is going next. We take a look at this from both the macro and micro levels because you'll need to understand and anticipate both in the coming months and years of Facebook.

Facebook is growing and changing at such a fast pace that by the time you get your hands on this book, there will be a few more changes. This is the third edition of the book, and substantial changes were required to keep it up to date. Facebook frequently releases new features and opportunities that you will be adapting long after you establish a firm foundation with this book. Buckle your seat belts, secure your tray tables, and return your chairs to their full upright position, and let's take a flight through Facebook.

Who Should Buy This Book

This book is for professionals who want to understand how Facebook can be integrated into their business, and for small business owners and corporate marketing professionals who want to market companies and brands via Facebook. This includes anyone from the CEO to the CMO to PR, communications, and marketing. Not only will you gain an understanding of how you can use Facebook within your business, you will be armed with the necessary information to prove its value to others within your company.

How This Book Is Organized

Facebook Marketing is organized into four parts:

Part I: Getting Started

Chapter 1, "Getting Around Facebook: The Basics," provides an introduction to the phenomenon known as Facebook and provides you with a foundation for going deeper into the platform and understanding how it can be integrated into your business.

Chapter 2, "Addressing Privacy Concerns," reviews the changes in Facebook's privacy policy over the years, how that affects your business, and what you need to know about your privacy, or the lack thereof, on Facebook. Because privacy on Facebook is something that affects personal profiles, business pages, applications and several other areas of the platform, we'll explore each of these and explain why this is important for your business to really understand.

Chapter 3, "Establishing a Corporate Presence," explores establishing a corporate presence with a Facebook Page, including designing custom landing tabs, leveraging the Events platform, measuring your performance, and much more. You gain an understanding of how to set up each of these features for your business, how they can be used, and which features you should select based on your business goals.

Part II: Intermediate Marketing Skills

Chapter 4, "Facebook Advertising: How and Why You Should Be Using It," you learn about the Facebook advertising platform and why you should use it. You learn how to create an ad, discover how many people within your target demographic are on Facebook, setting a budget, understanding CPC versus CPM, launching your campaign, and measuring it using Facebook Analytics and Insights.

Chapter 5, "Facebook Page Analytics: Tracking Your Success," shows you the deep data Facebook provides about your users and their interactions on your Facebook Pages, as well as how you can dive deeper with third-party solutions and Google Analytics.

Chapter 6, "Using Facebook to Develop Communities," explores how to make decisions about Group and Page strategies and what tactics you can use to build and nurture your communities.

Part III: Getting the Most Out of Advanced Facebook Features

Chapter 7, "The Power of Local: Facebook Places and Deals," provides you with a deeper understanding of Facebook's location-based features. This chapter explores how your business can best leverage locations and deals, and how this can benefit your business.

Chapter 8, "Socialize Your Website with Facebook Connect and Social Plugins," breaks out of the walled garden of Facebook.com and discusses integrating Facebook into websites using the Like button, chat, commenting, and other powerful features.

Chapter 9, "Facebook Credits: Social Currency and Your Business," digs into Facebook applications, not from the technical aspect, but from understanding how they can be utilized on your Facebook Page and what role applications have outside of Facebook. We will break down what Facebook Credits are and how virtual currency may be an essential monetization effort by Facebook. During this chapter we will also explain why virtual currency is a worthwhile option over real currency and how your business should be leveraging virtual currency.

Part IV: Role Models and Predictions

Because you're not the first company to jump into Facebook, Chapter 10, "Best in Class Facebook Pages," provides you with some of the best case studies of companies that have leveraged Facebook to build communities and engage with their audiences. These case studies are above and beyond those that are mentioned throughout the other chapters in the book.

Chapter 11, "What's Next for Facebook," looks into the crystal ball and tries to figure out what's next for Facebook. This is your sandbox to play in to see whether you can figure out where Facebook goes from here. Place your bets and let 'em ride!

Conventions Used in This Book

Special conventions are used to help you get the most from this book and from Facebook.

Special Elements

Throughout this book you'll find Tips, Tasks, Case Studies, Definitions, and side-bars. These elements provide a variety of information that will enrich your Face-book experience, but they aren't required reading.

 Tips

Tips are designed to point out features to help your experience with Facebook be smoother, more enjoyable and more productive. As with the early days in math class, you'll have to learn some of the hard ways first and then we'll teach you quick tips that will help you.

 Notes

Throughout the chapters are notes that will help you fully grasp the information being discussed and see how others have successfully utilized the features being highlighted in that particular chapter.

Endnotes

1. http://www.thecrimson.com/article/2003/11/19/facemash-creator-survives-ad-board-the/

2. http://en.wikipedia.org/wiki/History_of_Facebook

3. http://en.wikipedia.org/wiki/Timeline_of_Facebook

4. http://www.webpronews.com/facebook-sees-m-from-greylock-2006-04

5. http://www.nytimes.com/2007/10/25/technology/24cnd-facebook.html

6. http://www.facebook.com/press/releases.php?p=9176

7. http://www.facebook.com/press/info.php?statistics

Getting Started

1

Getting Around Facebook: The Basics

If you're new to Facebook or just considering whether to join, this chapter can help you to get up and running quickly. As Facebook continues to grow, and at the rate at which it's growing, at times it can be hard to keep up with all the updates, such as enhancements and new features. Although getting around Facebook isn't exactly hard, this chapter covers some of the basic tools and features.

If you're an experienced Facebook user, feel free to skim through this chapter or skip it entirely and go to the next chapter, where you'll learn about establishing a corporate presence.

What you won't find in this chapter is an exact step-by-step process. Actually, you won't find that anywhere throughout this book. You want actionable and descriptive information that can help you immediately, not a step-by-step tutorial.

Getting Started

First of all, congrats! If you're considering whether to join, if you just joined, or if you are an experienced user, you're part of one of the fastest growing and largest social networks in history. Millions of people share your same interests, hobbies, career goals, and just about anything else you can think of. To find all these friends, networking opportunities, and groups, you have to know how and where to look. You also have to take the time to invest in building your presence on Facebook.

Therefore, let's get you up and running as quickly as possible so that you can start reaping all the wonderful benefits that Facebook has to offer.

To start, go to www.facebook.com. When the page loads, you'll notice a section for new users to sign up, as shown in Figure 1.1. Pop in your basic information, click Sign Up, and we're off to the races.

Figure 1.1   *The Facebook landing page where you can either sign up for an account or log in to your account.*

After you register and log in to Facebook for the first time, you need to do a few things immediately.

0–60 on Facebook in 11 Steps

Let's get you started on Facebook. These 11 steps will help you get your personal profile up and running in about an hour:

1.   Take a Few Minutes to Familiarize Yourself

This is either a new world you're stepping into or a familiar social network you're
determined to spend more time hanging out on. It has lots of features, as shown
in Figure 1.2—many of which we discuss. Click around; you won't break anything.
(Well, hopefully you won't break anything.)

Figure 1.2   *After you log in to Facebook, you see the home page that serves as your
dashboard to access many of the features of your Facebook account.*

2.   Upload a Picture of Yourself

We want to see who you are. When someone searches for you, they're much more
likely to engage and recognize you if they're greeted with a nice picture. When you
do searches in Facebook, the search results provide you with only those people's
pictures, names, and networks. Therefore, it can be hard to identify people you're
looking for if they don't have a picture uploaded, especially if it's a common name.
For this reason, uploading a profile photo is a must. Besides, one of the reasons
you're probably hanging out on Facebook, besides using it for your marketing
needs, is to have meaningful personal relationships. Pictures help really well with
that. On the marketing side, a photo helps to humanize your brand. It allows your
prospects, customers, and fans to connect directly with you and know exactly who
they are talking to.

Please don't post anything offensive. Facebook isn't the right place for offensive
pictures, and Facebook actively polices the network. At a basic level, why would
you even want to upload a picture that was offensive to a network that you don't
control and in a world where everything you do becomes a permanent record?

Do post a picture of yourself that shows your personality. The most preferred type of photo to upload as your profile picture is a nice one of you by yourself, either a head shot or a full body picture. This allows the focus to be on you, and people don't have to guess which person you might be. Also, remember that the profile picture in search results and other areas of the network appear much smaller. If other people, animals, or objects are in the photo, it will make it harder to distinguish what's going on and which person in the photo you are. But some people don't want to be found or recognized in search, so in that case, have fun uploading a shot of an animal or a place instead.

Uploading group pictures as your profile picture should be a no-no, because it will be nearly impossible to see you in it, especially if someone has never seen a photo of you or met you before.

3.   Fill Out Your Profile

We know this seems time-consuming, but this is one of the main ways that people can find you. It's the quickest way for me to get to know you when you accept my friendship request. Also, some of the ever-increasing applications created for Facebook can leverage some of this information to help keep contact lists up to date, such as on the iPhone, Palm Pre, and Android platforms.

Some of the information you have the option to enter—and that you will be prompted to fill in, as shown in Figure 1.3, includes the following: sex, birthday, home town, relationship status, type of connections you want to establish, interests, favorite music, favorite TV shows, favorite movies, favorite books, quotations, a little information about yourself, contact information, and your education and work background.

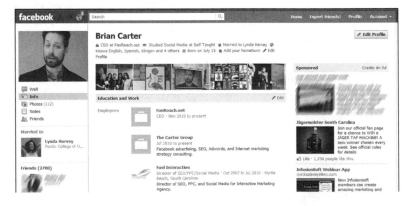

Figure 1.3 *The Info tab of your Facebook account contains all the basic information you choose to share about yourself.*

Now, you don't have to fill ALL this out; you should answer only questions that you feel comfortable with having posted. If you don't want to display your full contact info, that's understandable. If you prefer not to mention your political preference, don't. But do take the time to share as much as you're comfortable with.

 Tip

> If you're a married woman who has changed her name, consider including your maiden name so that old friends and family can more easily find you. Remember, they might not know that you're married.

By the time this book reaches the printer, Facebook may have moved the new Timeline Profile from beta to mainstream usage. Figure 1.4 shows what it looks like.

Figure 1.4   *The new Timeline profile.*

As Mark Zuckerberg put it when he introduced Timeline in September 2011 at the F8 conference, it's "The Story of Your Life In One Page." It's much more visual and historical than the old profile. It's like *Time* Magazine's Year In Review infographic, but applied to your life. And you can choose each element so it displays your life to the world the way you want. And you can choose privacy settings so that groups of people see what you want them to see.

Currently, you get a week to play with your Timeline before it's published, or you can publish as soon as you have it where you want it.

The first thing you choose is your Cover, which is a big masthead photo that represents a unique moment in your life. To change your cover, hover over the cover photo, and click on change cover. Then you'll get a pop-up of photos and you can choose to dive into your albums to look for the right picture. You may want to try several before you figure out which photo works best at that size and how your want to represent yourself. The question is, should it be a professional moment? A personal one? Your family? Your wedding? It really depends on how you use your profile on a daily basis.

The View Activity button takes you to a private log of all your posts and activity, since your first action on Facebook. You can change the privacy setting for any post or story, delete posts, and more.

You can use the Time Slider to change the date you're looking at, and you can star, hide or delete anything you see below (see Figure 1.5).

Figure 1.5 *Scrolling down, you see various stories in the Timeline, and you can hide stories or tell Facebook which ones they should feature.*

4.   Start Finding Some Friends

The main way in which you connect with people on Facebook is through *friending* them. These people can be family, friends, colleagues, business partners, or people who want to connect for a variety of other reasons. There is no "right" number for the total number of friends you should have. You shouldn't focus on the number.

Be focused on finding interesting people, many of whom you already know, and connect with them as often as possible. Facebook provides a perfect platform for relationship development, personal and professional networking, and connecting with old friends, family, and colleagues.

As Nick O'Neill of AllFacebook.com points out: "One of the biggest challenges on Facebook is the loss of new users that are not able to connect immediately with other members." However, you can find people to connect with on Facebook in a number of ways. The following are just a few of the ways, but if you use these, it can definitely help to get you up to speed.

If you use one of the more popular email services, such as Gmail or Yahoo!, head on over to the Friend Finder section, as shown in Figure 1.6. When you're new, Facebook bugs you with this option. If you have trouble finding it, go to www.facebook.com/find friends/. Pop in your email and password. (Don't worry; Facebook isn't selling it to some foreign country.) Facebook searches the people you communicate with via email and spits back a list of people it finds who are on Facebook. Easy cheesy.

Figure 1.6   *The Friend Finder section, where you can enter your email information and Facebook will search your address book to find people who you communicate with who also have a Facebook account.*

If you use a work email service that pops through Outlook, iMail, Entourage, or another desktop email software, never fear! Scroll down to Other Tools, click Find Friends, then Upload Contact File, and, as shown in Figure 1.7, you can upload your contact file. This can also be done through the Friend Finder section.

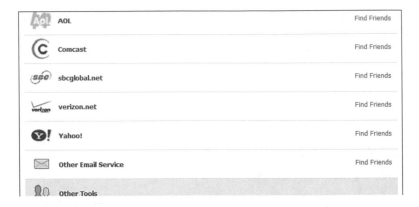

Figure 1.7 *If you don't use one of the popular email services such as Gmail or Yahoo! to manage your contacts, or if you prefer to keep your address book outside of email services, you can upload a contact file to the Friend Finder as well.*

5. **Import Your AOL Instant Messenger (AIM) or Windows Live Buddies**

Figure 1.6 shows a list of some of the many email services you can use to find your friends on Facebook. Click on "Find Friends" next to the email service you use, then enter your login info (which Facebook will not save), and follow the process from there to identify friends from your email contacts.

Based on the educational and work information you input into your profile, Facebook creates saved searches. For example, you can click to run a search for everyone who graduated high school or college with you. Alternatively, you can also go directly to your profile and click the name of your school or company to run that search.

You can also use the Friend Browser (see Figure 1.8). If you can't find it, go to www.facebook.com/find-friends/browser/. This allows you to find friends by city, school name, company, and other factors.

Finally, you can run an advanced search from the search box at the top of every page. After you're on the search results page, click People in the left nav. You can also get to this search page by going to www.facebook.com/search.php (see Figure 1.9).

Running searches is the most manual of the processes, but it is the one you use the most after you run through the preceding steps.

Figure 1.8   *Using the Friend Browser, you can search for friends, family, or colleagues by searching based on their email address, school, or company.*

Figure 1.9   *You can search all Facebook users by name and location.*

As your friends begin to accept your friend requests, Facebook asks them to make friend suggestions to help you grow your network. This can happen only in the beginning until Facebook senses that you have developed a strong network.

As you continue to grow your network, Facebook provides you with friend suggestions based on mutual friends you might share, similar interests, and such. This can be a great way to connect with people who you might be following on other networks and through the previously mentioned methods, when you still haven't found each other.

6. Upload More Photos

Uploading a profile photo or two isn't enough. We want to learn more about you. We want to see more than just that headshot and the basic information you provided. One of the ways that you can do that is through creating albums and uploading photos to Facebook.

Go through and pick out a handful of your favorite photos and create your first photo albums on Facebook. Many people, including both of us, go straight to people's photos as the quickest way to learn more about them. We like to see where you've been, you having fun with your family, joking around at the office, or anything else you're willing to share.

Facebook makes it easy to upload a lot of pictures at once by allowing you to browse your computer's hard drive and select all photos or grab a specific selection. Facebook also gives you the ability to upload directly from your phone; or if you're a Mac user, you can use iPhoto, as well.

As you grow your list of friends, you can go back through and "tag" any friends of yours who appear in your photos, too (see Figure 1.10). Warning: This can become addictive.

Figure 1.10   *The tagging feature within Facebook photos.*

7. Upload a Video or Two

Do you have a short video that you shot on vacation, during the holidays, or last Friday night when you were out with friends? Throw it up there. Because we might never have met in real life, uploading photos and videos is the way that we can connect with you and match your personality with the words that are on the screen.

Don't have any videos? Start creating 'em. Use a webcam, iSight (if you're a Mac owner), your phone, your digital camera, or Flip camera, and start capturing some of the mayhem that you're causing. Just like photos, you can tag your friends in videos as well.

As a piece of advice, try to keep the video under 3–5 minutes. Everyone is really busy, and the longer you make the video, the less likely people are to watch it, share it, or maybe even blog about it. Keep it short and fun!

8. Send Your First Status Using the Publisher Tool

Updating your status is how we know what you're up to, what you're thinking, and how you'll share anything you find interesting, such as ideas, links, photos, videos, and questions. You certainly don't need to update your status 487 times per day. In fact, although it's considered ideal to post 20+ times a day on Twitter, a few times per day is perfect for Facebook. (See Figure 1.11 for an example.)

Figure 1.11   *The Publisher tool within Facebook—your primary communications tool to share information. You can even create polls for your friends to vote on.*

Updating your status can help you to stay top-of-mind with friends as your status jumps into the News Feed, giving your friends the chance to leave comments and Like or Share the stuff you're putting in.

9. Download a Facebook Mobile Application

Are you part of the ever-increasing population that's using a smartphone, such as an iPhone (see Figure 1.12), a BlackBerry, a Palm Pre, or an Android-platform device? If so, grab the Facebook app made for your device.

Figure 1.12 *The official Facebook App on the iPhone.*

Alternatively, you can use the mobile version of Facebook by heading over to m.facebook.com. This allows you to easily add new content, such as photos and videos, update your status, see what you're friends are up to, and access a number of other features while you're on the go. If it weren't for the mobile app, our Facebook usage would be much lower than what it is. It allows us to constantly produce content and share what we're up to, even if we're away from a laptop or Internet connection.

10. Start Interacting with Your Friends

Facebook gives you this great opportunity to connect with friends, colleagues, and people you meet. Take advantage of it. Cruise around and look at the photos and videos your friends upload. Check out some links your friends share. Leave a comment or two; share something they've said or "Like" a few things. But, a word of caution—please don't "own" your friends' Facebook accounts. There is no need to comment or Like everything that they post. This will not only become annoying but also can start to seem disingenuous. Comment on a couple items per day and you'll be on the road to success.

11.   Have Fun and Explore!

The most important thing you can do is try to have fun. If you're not having fun, you're less likely to use it. That's definitely not what any of us want to happen. You're reading this book to find how you can leverage Facebook better person-ally and professionally. If you don't have fun with the basic steps, everything that comes after will make you want to run around with scissors. Not that there's any-thing wrong with that.

Take some time, get used to how things work around Facebook, and have fun. It can eat up a lot of your time if you let it, but that's okay. Remember that this is all about making connections, interacting, and building or strengthening trust. The only way any of that can happen is if you put in time, have fun, and are genu-ine throughout the entire process. Besides, it's not really "eating up your time" as much as it is making an investment in your future by allowing you a way to develop personal and professional relationships with others.

Although these 11 steps certainly don't cover everything that you will find yourself doing when you first sign up, they can have you feeling right at home sooner than later.

Now that we have your profile filled out and you've uploaded a few pictures and maybe a video, and you're starting to get friend requests, we should go over a few of the basic features and tools.

Home Page News Feed and Ticker

When you first log in to Facebook, you are directed to your home page, as shown in Figure 1.13. This page can be accessed at any time by clicking Home on the top toolbar. The home page is your real-time News Feed of what your friends share on Facebook. All their status updates and anything they choose to share, such as pho-tos, videos, new applications, and so on appear here.

By default, the News Feed is a blend of Top Stories and Recent Stories. Facebook uses an algorithm called EdgeRank to determine Top Stories—they come from the friends and pages you interact with most. You will see more of the types of posts (statuses, photos, videos, and questions) you interact with, and less of those you don't.

The News Ticker in the upper-right hand corner constantly scrolls in new activity from friends and pages. You can hover over any of these and Facebook will show blow up any attached picture to show you more (as seen in Figure 1.13).

Figure 1.13   *The home page showing the News Feed, Ticker, and other features in the left sidebar.*

Besides the news stream running down the center of the page, you have a lot of other options in the left sidebar. You'll see News Feed, Messages, Events, and Friends. Then you'll see Groups, if you're in any. Below that, your options are customized by Facebook to show what you use most.

The home page is valuable because it serves as your dashboard into Facebook. If you don't have a lot of time on a given day, the home page allows you to jump in quickly, see what's going on, maybe make a few comments, accept a couple friend requests, wish a friend Happy Birthday, and then get out.

Keep in mind that other people can see the actions you take on Facebook. Change your relationship status before remembering to tell your now ex-significant other? Yup, everyone else will see before he or she knows. Did you just Like a page you don't want everyone to know you like? It will post to the News Feed. But relax—you can change that! Click the link in the upper right to your Profile, and you'll see all those kinds of posts. Click the down arrow in the upper right of the kind of post you don't want people to see, and you'll see a menu that allows you to hide that type of activity. We'll go over more privacy options in Chapter 2, "Addressing Privacy Concerns."

The News Feed also gives users the ability to jump in and comment or "Like," in real-time, what their friends are posting. The home page/news feed creates a real-time two-way communications channel, thus increasing user engagement with others and with the tool.

Comments and Likes

One of the nice features of commenting and likes is notification, when others jump in and comment on or Like that particular update. This allows for that back-and-forth communications channel that we've been talking about.

If you don't have a comment to leave but found the update interesting, you can choose to simply "Like" the update, which essentially means giving it a thumbs up.

Publisher Tool

When you click the Profile tab at the top of your window, you'll be brought to your profile. Click on Update Status to bring up a box you can type in (It will ask you "What's On Your Mind?"). This is called the Publisher tool within Facebook, and it serves as your main portal to sharing information with your network (see Figure 1.14).

Figure 1.14   *Using the Publisher tool to send a status update that will be dropped into the general news feed based on my preferences.*

The Publisher tool initially started out as a field to update your status. But as the platform grew, Facebook updated it to support the sharing of videos, photos, events, smart links, and more options. (Facebook automatically scans a link to pull a title, description, and photo from the site you're sharing, as shown in Figure 1.15.)

Figure 1.15   *Adding a link into the Publisher tool. This example shows a blog post from which Facebook automatically pulled in an image, the title, and excerpt.*

The Publisher tool allows you to control the privacy settings around status updates made through the tool (see Figure 1.16). Previous to this enhancement, any status you posted would be public to everyone. But, with the new updates, you now have a choice to make your status updates visible to everyone, your network and friends, friends of friends, only friends, or a customized list.

We address privacy issues in greater detail in Chapter 2, but the update to the Publisher tool was one of biggest steps Facebook made in giving users more privacy controls.

Photos

The photo feature within Facebook is probably the platform's most-used feature. More than 1 billion photos are uploaded and shared on Facebook every month. This makes Facebook the top photo-sharing site in the world.

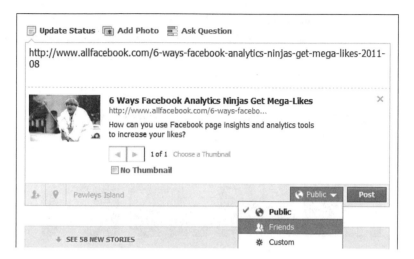

Figure 1.16   *Some of the privacy settings you can choose for posts.*

So what is it that makes everyone go so crazy over photos? It is probably the ease with which you can upload them. In a few clicks you can gain access to your entire photo library on your hard drive, and you can begin uploading everything into customized photo albums that you have defined within Facebook. Each photo album can hold only 200 photos, which is far better than the previous limit of approximately 70. But, if you just came back from vacation and have a few hundred pictures that you want to upload, you need to create several albums.

When you upload photos to Facebook, you have the option of publishing a preview of these pictures to your Wall, which will also drop them into the news stream. This is a great way to alert your network that you have uploaded new photos you want them to check out.

In addition to uploading and sharing pictures, you can tag your friends in the pictures that you upload. For the tag feature, they must be Facebook users and friends of yours. When you tag friends, Facebook automatically sends them a notice that they've been tagged in a photo and, depending on their privacy settings, it posts that photo onto their Wall and into the Photos area below their main photo, as well in the photos at the top of their profile (see Figure 1.17).

However, privacy concerns have been raised over the tagging of photos, which we discuss more in Chapter 2. Suffice it to say though, you shouldn't be uploading anything to Facebook that you're nervous about ANYONE else seeing, whether or not they're your friend on the network. You can remove people's ability to tag you in photos in your privacy settings, and you can remove tags from photos you don't want to be tagged in. We'll also talk about Profile Review in the Chapter 2, which allows you to review all posts you're tagged in.

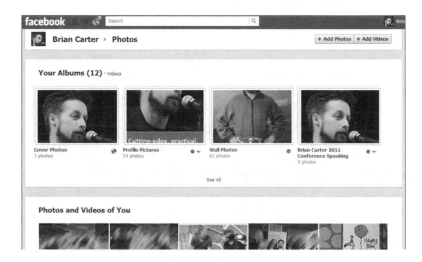

Figure 1.17   *The Photos option from your Timeline shows albums of photos you've uploaded, plus pictures of you uploaded by friends.*

Videos

Similar to the photo feature, Facebook allows you to upload, share, and tag videos. If you tag yourself or are tagged in a video, it appears in the Videos subsection of your Photos section.

Facebook provides the option of uploading a video from your hard drive or recording directly into Facebook from your webcam (see Figure 1.18). Although videos are not as popular as photos, more than 20 million videos were uploaded to Facebook per month in 2010, and more than 2 billion videos are *watched* per month on Facebook.

One of the reasons videos probably aren't as popular is that we're just starting to see phones that can capture and upload video. However, with digital cameras that can capture quality video, and devices such as the Flip, we believe the use of video on Facebook will continue to grow.

But videos may never be as popular as photos, because a video whose quality people feel comfortable with is harder and more time-consuming to create than a good photo. We'd say the average amateur cellphone photographer is better than the average amateur cellphone videographer, wouldn't you?

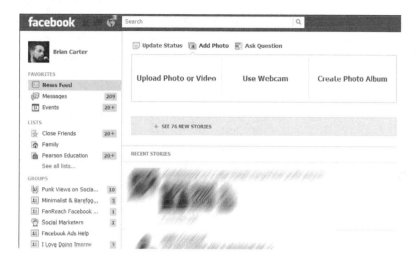

Figure 1.18   *Click Add Photo, and you can either upload a video or record a video directly into Facebook with your webcam.*

If you're creating a lot of video, you might want to look into TubeMogul's OneLoad service, which allows you to upload the video once and push it out to multiple video networks. That means that you can upload a video to TubeMogul and push it out to Facebook, YouTube, Viddler, Blip.tv, Vimeo, and 20 other video networks at once.

Pages and Groups

Facebook provides the option to build, find, and be part of communities built around topics, products, brands, celebrities, and just about anything else you can think of. Do a search for some of your favorite hobbies, bands, or companies. If they have a presence on Facebook, consider becoming a *fan*. Not only will you be joining a community of like-minded folks who you can interact with in a variety of ways, but it'll also be added to your profile so that other people can see where you like to hang out on Facebook and what you're interested in.

In Chapter 3, "Establishing a Corporate Presence," we discuss how you can create a successful Page or Group for your company, service, or product, including how to properly gain exposure, cultivate the community, and leverage your fans to help spread your message.

Notes

One application some people take extensive advantage of is called Notes. Facebook says, "With Facebook Notes, you can share your life with your friends through written entries. You can tag your friends in notes, and they can leave comments." This might seem similar to the blog feature in MySpace that a lot of people used but that never quite resonated the way the MySpace team intended. You can see your friends' notes by going to www.facebook.com/notes/. If you haven't used Notes much, you might have to click More in the left navigation to find it.

Facebook Notes are used by some people as an alternative to a blogging platform, although it isn't recommend because there are much better professional platforms such as WordPress, MoveableType, and TypePad. Others use Notes to post stories about friends that they can then tag or things that they find that are interesting (see Figure 1.19).

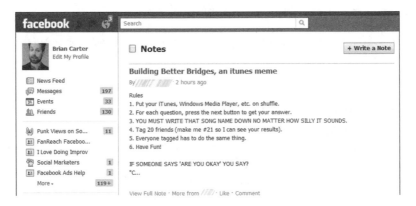

Figure 1.19   *Notes is a longer format for sharing ideas with Facebook friends.*

Facebook Chat

When Facebook originally launched, it was during a time when instant messaging was becoming a primary communication tool for many high school and college students. Facebook users would stop by Facebook to post a status update, upload a few photos, or check in on their friends, but they still did the bulk of their communicating using other tools such as AIM, Yahoo! IM, Google Talk, and so on.

Although Facebook didn't face any competition from these services as far as feature offerings, Facebook still wants to keep users on its page as long as possible. The longer users stay on the Facebook site, the more likely they are to share, take a few more minutes to upload that batch of photos, or search for a few more friends.

With that in mind, Facebook launched Facebook Chat, its instant messaging tool. Facebook Chat enables you to instantly message and chat with any of your friends who are logged into Facebook. From the chat window, which resides in the right-most part of your window (see Figure 1.20), you can launch into that user's profile.

Figure 1.20   *Facebook Chat used within Facebook. You can also use Facebook Chat in IM aggregator services such as Meebo.*

As Facebook Chat has continued to grow, several instant messaging applications have been created to help users consolidate their various IM services into one tool (such as Adium, Jabber, and Meebo).

Search

As Facebook gained more and more users, it became clear that the standard search feature would not be enough. Originally, Facebook Search allowed you to search only for people, Groups, or Pages based on name only. Any of the information that was entered in status updates, for example, was not searchable. This was the largest edge that Twitter had over Facebook.

With Twitter Search (http://search.twitter.com), users can search the conversations taking place on the network in real time. Users can grab customized RSS feeds based on the search criteria, and then those can be transferred into a feed reader such as Google Reader (www.google.com/reader). For a long time, Facebook took criticism because it didn't have a more robust search engine, especially because Facebook has hundreds of millions of users compared to tens of millions using Twitter.

In June 2009, Facebook announced that it was experimenting with an enhanced search feature (see Figure 1.21) to help users mine through the tons of information that pumps into the platform daily. Approximately two months later, Facebook released the new search feature. In 2010, Facebook served results for 500 million search queries per day, and that number continues to grow.

Figure 1.21   *The search feature used to search for mentions of Cowboys and Aliens among my friends and pages. You can also search everyone on Facebook or posts in Groups you belong to.*

The search engine optimization (SEO) industry is a $19 billion dollar industry in 2011, and the hardcore folks who write the SEO blogs and speak at SEO conferences (which include me, Brian) have begun to talk seriously about optimizing for Facebook Search. This area will only continue to grow.

A few other websites can help you search Facebook. The two most interesting to me are Greplin and OpenBook. Greplin (greplin.com) does a great job of being your personal, private social search utility after you give it access to your social streams (see Figure 1.22). Brian uses it to search his Facebook, Twitter, and LinkedIn all at one time. OpenBook was originally created to show how few people realized their status updates were public. It also can be useful for brand research.

Figure 1.22 *After you join Greplin and give it access, it enables you to search all your social profiles and friends.*

Managing Friends and Friend Lists

The Friends option allows you to segment your friends into different lists, as shown in Figure 1.23. This is helpful especially when you get past having a handful of friends. You can classify your friends into any list you determine in addition to some of the basic lists/searches that Facebook already has set up for you. This is useful especially with the enhanced privacy features for status updates and the sharing of information. If you've created segmented lists, you can choose to share certain updates, photos, or information with only a particular list. That means that your college buddies don't have to see the industry news that you want to share with your professional contacts, if you don't want them to. It also means your boss doesn't get to see your Vegas photos.

A lot of people like to specify who their family is, as well, which you can do by going to Profile and clicking Edit Profile (see Figure 1.24). You can even list an expected child now, if you want. Make sure you customize who can see your family relationships in your Privacy Settings.

Figure 1.23 *The Manage Friends area, where you can create different lists to enable you to filter your friends quickly.*

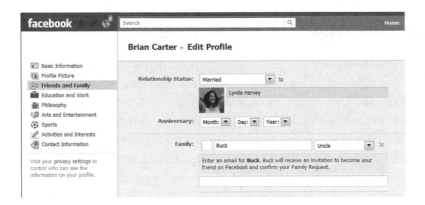

Figure 1.24 *Adding to your family list in the Edit Profile section.*

Messages

Facebook, like many other social networks, has its own private messaging system. This can be accessed via the Inbox tab at the top of your screen. From there, you can send Facebook email to any one of your friends (see Figure 1.25). Facebook also allows you to attach links, photos, videos, or other application updates (depending on the actual application), similar to the Publisher tool.

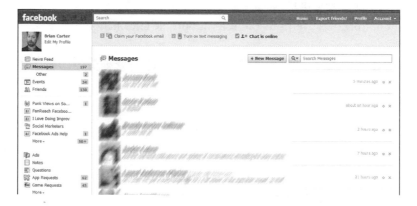

Figure 1.25   *The Facebook Inbox, where users can message each other and Groups or Pages administrators can send messages to their communities.*

This messaging is now integrating with Chat. You'll notice that when you chat with someone, the messages will show up in your Messages area as well. There's also an Other inbox that few people ever look at. This is where messages from Pages go. That's good and bad; if you're a Page administrator, you're better off posting to your fans' News Feed, but the good news is that as a user, you see less spam than in normal email. You can integrate messages with email as well, if you like.

There has been some discussion in the blogosphere about whether Facebook's messaging system will make normal email obsolete. We think this is unlikely, because many companies won't want to give up domain-branded emails such as Brian@ FanReach.net, and because even in the countries where Facebook is most popular, not everyone who's online is on Facebook.

Account Settings

In Account Settings, you control many aspects of your Facebook account (see Figure 1.26): You can select what you want to be shared from your profile and with whom. There are many settings under this area, and you should take some time tweaking these settings to your liking.

- Set your vanity URL (username).
- Specify types of notifications you want to receive and how you want to receive them.

- Edit the level of access apps have to your account, or delete apps.
- Set up mobile messaging.
- Pay for Facebook Credits.
- Control how advertisers can use your profile information.

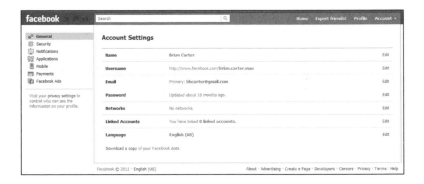

Figure 1.26 *The Account Settings feature allows you to control nearly every aspect of your Facebook account.*

The goal of this book is marketing with Facebook and is not meant to be an all encompassing reference to using Facebook. Therefore, we haven't covered every single feature in Facebook—it is the features described in this chapter that run throughout the entire platform. It is important to understand how this framework contributes to Facebook.

2

Addressing Privacy Concerns

Throughout this book, you will be encouraged to take advantage of the many features available in Facebook. Knowing that you've been a good student, you've now filled in your city, state, phone number, marital status, uploaded photos, tagged videos, and linked your notes together. The marketer side of you will perk up in the next chapter to create a Page and/or Group and link that to your profile. Maybe you thought about the amount of personal and professional information you're sharing. Maybe not. Maybe you have taken the time to review the Terms of Service and Privacy Policy. But, chances are, like every other Terms of Service or Privacy Policy, you haven't bothered to look. Have you thought of the ways in which these policies can affect your ability to market your brand, product, or service? Have you considered where all that information that you share is visible? Can Google and the other search engines see all that information? Should you keep your personal account separate from these marketing activities? Can you even do that? These are all questions that fly around the interwebs when people discuss privacy concerns and Facebook.

As Facebook continues to grow, it is becoming less and less a purely personal network. It's not the network you go to just to relax at the end of the day and catch up with a few friends or check out family photos. Nowadays, many people use Facebook as part of their online reputation management and personal/professional branding strategy. People use Facebook for both personal and professional connections and networking. As Facebook grows larger and people continue to blur the line between personal and professional, concerns over privacy continue to grow.

Privacy within Facebook needs to be addressed on multiple levels:

- The sharing of personal information and whether, because of that, you should use Facebook as a professional tool as well.

- How to properly configure the privacy settings for both your personal profile and any Pages or Groups you administer and manage.

- What the Terms of Service and Privacy Policy actually allow you to do within Facebook.

- How all this ties together and affects marketers trying to use Facebook as part of their marketing strategy for their brand, product, or service.

All these issues are addressed throughout the next few pages.

The Two Faces of Privacy on Facebook

Because Facebook started out as a personal network, it has been a hard transition for people to become used to it as a professional network. Originally, most people used LinkedIn as a professional network and Facebook as a personal network. But with the growth rate of Facebook, many began to turn to it as a personal branding tool and professional network. Marketers turned to Facebook with Facebook Pages, Groups, and advertisements as a way to reach out to their prospects, customers, and fans.

This transition created a dilemma for many folks because they resisted using Facebook as a professional network, yet their colleagues, competition, and companies were becoming active on the network. Also, as we develop friends in our industries, we want to extend that friendship and therefore turn to Facebook. This starts to blur that line even further between work and home. However, as Dawn Foster of WebWorkerDaily points out, we don't want to confuse "personal" for "private":

"You can actually be professional and personal at the same time in social media without too much effort. When we talk about 'being personal' on social media websites, we think that many people confuse 'personal' with 'private.' The reality is that you get to decide what to share and what not to share, so you can still keep most areas of your private life private."

To deal with this dilemma, individuals typically have three options to choose from:

- A single Facebook profile that combines personal and professional.
- Two different Facebook profiles: one personal and one professional.
- Keeping Facebook personal only and not mixing work into it.

Each one of these has both upsides and downsides with no clear answer or best practice, as of yet. Although it might not be clear yet, this will be important for you as a marketer or company. Let's explore each of these options.

Single Facebook Profile

You can use a personal profile for business networking purposes, but if you go over the line in the mind of any friend, they could report you to Facebook. If you try to friend too many people who don't know you, you can likewise be reported, and your ability to request new friends may be disabled by Facebook.

If you don't mind mixing the personal and the professional, you can maintain a single Facebook profile in which all engagement with the platform originates from that one profile. This enables people to get to know the real you. It's just like the two faces that most wear on a daily basis: the way you are at your office and the way you are at home, with friends or family.

Although so many of us are used to this split personality, why should we act like this? Why can't we be the same person at work as we are at home, maybe just dressed up a little nicer? You have the same likes and dislikes, the same problems and victories, and your family, friends, enemies, colleagues, and competitors don't change when you're at work versus when you're at home (see Figure 2.1).

Furthermore, realizing its growth, Facebook has continued to add features that allow you to tweak your privacy settings to allow you to use a single profile but limit access to data sets based on permissions, lists, and rules that you set up. This means that you can create a list of your colleagues and then deny that list access to certain aspects of your profile. By setting this up properly, you can achieve the privacy and separation that you want while not having to bother with two separate profiles or avoiding Facebook as a professional network.

Figure 2.1 *Mixing professional promotion and personal thoughts, Brian uses his Facebook profile for a blend of professional and personal uses.*

Two Different Facebook Profiles? Or Get a Page?

Some want to maintain separate personas, split between personal and professional lives, so they decide to create two different Facebook profiles.

Before you do this—indeed, before you do anything on Facebook—you should read the Facebook policies. In Facebook's Statement of Rights and Responsibilities (section 4.2), it's made crystal clear that "you will not create more than one personal profile." If you violate this, or any of its policies, know that Facebook could deactivate your accounts at any time.

If you are a solo entrepreneur, author, speaker, or some other personality-based business, you may consider creating a Facebook page for those business purposes. This keeps business and personal separate. But this is complicated by changes in late 2011 which made it possible for non-friends to "Subscribe" to your profile updates. You have to opt-in to make your profile subscribable. It's an interesting option for solo businesspeople—Kevin Rose of Digg has more than 200,000 subscribers to his profile!

Not Doing Business on Facebook

Your last option is to not mix work with Facebook. Some people maintain Facebook as their personal social network and use LinkedIn as their professional network to connect with colleagues. For those wanting to maintain that separation between personal and work, you might find this to be your cleanest option.

Privacy Settings

Understanding and tweaking the privacy settings for both personal profiles and for any Pages and Groups you manage is important. (For more about this, see Chapter 3, "Establishing a Corporate Presence.") Otherwise, you might expose, share, or allow others to share information about you or your brand that you don't want shared, at least not without your permission.

Although it's not one of the most fun things to do within Facebook, you need to take some time and walk through each of the settings.

Personal Privacy Settings

If you haven't done so already, spend some time going through the privacy settings and configuring them based on your comfort with exposing personal information or other data and to whom you want to expose that information.

To begin configuring your privacy settings, click Account in the top navigation menu. One of the options under the drop-down menu is Privacy Settings. After you select the Privacy Settings option, you see a main privacy settings area in which you can control the privacy settings surrounding the following (see Figure 2.2):

- How you connect with friends
- How friends can tag you or your content
- What's shared with apps and websites
- Who can see past posts
- Block Lists

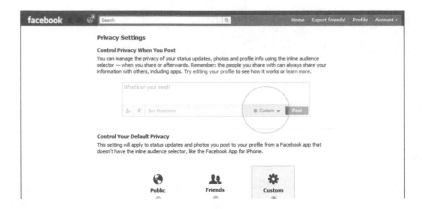

Figure 2.2   *The first privacy screen you see in Facebook.*

You can control your posts' default privacy setting: Public, Friends, or Custom. You can always change each post's actual privacy setting before you post it, and after you've changed it, it will remain on your latest setting. Make sure you check your post privacy setting before each post.

If you click on Edit Settings next to How You Connect, you'll see the dialog shown Figure 2.3, where you can control how people can or cannot connect with you, look you up, send you requests and messages, post on your wall, or see other people's wall posts on your profile.

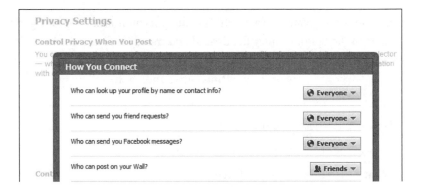

Figure 2.3   *Customizing how people can connect with you.*

Tagging is a feature Facebook dramatically expanded in August 2011. Previously used only for photos, Facebook expanded tagging privacy controls to include location and friend tagging. Figure 2.4 shows your tagging privacy options.

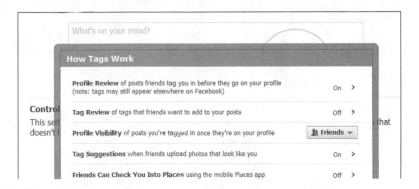

Figure 2.4 *Tagging privacy controls.*

Your friends may tag you in posts or photos. Profile Review allows you to moderate these tags before they go live on Facebook. Tag Suggestions is an interesting feature that allows Facebook to use its facial recognition technology to suggest friends tag you if it looks like you're in one of their photos.

But as we have learned throughout this book, the power of Facebook isn't just in what you can do within the walls of Facebook, but what you can interact with outside of Facebook using your profile, Facebook Connect, and applications. For this reason, Facebook allows you to control the privacy settings surrounding applications and websites that communicate with Facebook using your profile information, as shown in Figure 2.5. Under these settings you're able to control

- What you share
- What your friends can share about you—information such as your birthday, videos, photos, shared links, hometown, education, and other profile data
- Blocked applications
- Ignore application invites

After you've been on Facebook for any length of time, if you've installed apps, you might want to go back and remove the ones you don't use and double-check that they don't have more access to your data than you thought. If you click through to the application settings page, you'll be able to click each application to see the level of access they have (see Figure 2.6).

Figure 2.5 *Control access to your data by Facebook apps, friends' apps, games, and search.*

Figure 2.6 *Check on the level of access apps have to your data. Note that some are required by the app, but you can remove others and still use the app. Or, you can delete the app from your profile entirely.*

Although the preceding options are important to control valuable pieces of information, the exposure of your profile to search engines in 2007 drove a lot of controversy, so much so that it prompted Facebook to issue the following privacy announcement concerning the update, as shown in Figure 2.7.

Worried about search engines? Your information is safe. There have been misleading rumors recently about Facebook indexing all of your information on Google. This is not true. Facebook created Public Search listings in 2007 to enable people to search for your name and see a link to your Facebook profile. They will only see a basic set of information.

Figure 2.7   *Facebook shows you a preview of what search engines record and show to searchers. You can turn off Public Search to prevent people from seeing this.*

The last option in the Apps, Games, and Websites screen (not shown in Figure 2.7) is Public Search. You can preview what your profile looks like in the search engines (see Figure 2.7) and even turn off Public Search if you don't want it to show up there.

The final privacy section from Figure 2.2 is Block Lists. You can block people (see Figure 2.8), app invites from specific people, event invites from specific people and apps. You might want to block people who were offensive or are acting like stalkers. You can block invites from people who constantly ask you to use apps and go to events you don't care about.

Figure 2.8   *Is there someone that you don't want to find you on Facebook, but you don't want to restrict your profile to everyone? Under the Block settings, you can block people based on profile name and email.*

If you're considering blocking a person, you might worry about whether they'll know and if there might be repercussions from doing so. When you block someone, they are not notified of the blocking. However, they will no longer be able to view your profile and you won't appear in their search results or friend lists. They will become invisible to you as well. It will be, to them, as if you left Facebook completely. But obviously, in a true stalker situation, if the person knows about blocking, the stalker might be able to figure out you've blocked him or her. Make sure the police and people you care about know about the situation, and consider with them whether blocking might make things worse.

You can block apps that are aggressive in how they post to people's walls. For example, Brian and many others have blocked an app called BranchOut that is ostensibly a valuable career networking tool, but when you join, it posts marketing messages to *all* of your friends' walls. Many friends find this annoying. This is the only app we know to be this aggressive, and most people regard it as spammy. Also, LinkedIn blocked this app for violating its terms of service, so we feel comfortable with this blocking decision.

Why is it so important to ensure that you carefully go through all these settings? If you consider what we previously discussed about the potential option to maintain both your personal and professional lives from the same profile, you might want the ability to control who can see what. Additionally, you can control the ability of others to tag photos or videos of you and write on your Wall. If you don't, it is possible that even if you choose not to upload pictures or videos from a holiday party or weekend night out, someone else might, and they can tag you in them. Whether you did anything wrong isn't the only reason to be concerned. You might just want to control what aspects of your personal life your colleagues can see, and vice versa.

As a marketer, you need to pay special attention to the choice to expose data to public search engines. As we reviewed, any information marked as available to Everyone will be indexed by search engines. This can be important for gaining a few extra links for your company through exposing your, and your staff's, work information on your personal profiles. Also, if you're an independent or freelance marketer or trying to position yourself for the next big jump, you might want to expose particular aspects of your profile so that recruiters running background searches, general searches, or doing research can find you among those results.

However, it's not only the privacy settings that you can control that are important, but also the Privacy Policies and Terms of Services that Facebook implements for its users. These policies can have a profound affect on how you use Facebook for yourself and your company, product, or service.

Extensive Profile Privacy Settings

In August 2011, Facebook moved most of the privacy settings that have to do with your profile information into the Edit Profile section. To find it, click on Profile in the upper-right menu area, then click on the Update Info button. You'll see in Figure 2.9 that each piece of information now has a privacy control.

Figure 2.9   *To control which of your profile information is visible to whom, go to your Edit Profile section.*

You can even see exactly what your profile looks like to specific friends or family. Click on the menu with the gear icon and then on "View As..." In Figure 2.10, you can see what Brian's profile looks like to his wife.

Pages Privacy Settings

Now that you've spent some time adjusting the privacy settings of your personal profile, it is time to turn your attention to your Facebook Page. Although the number of settings to be adjusted and tweaked isn't as many as those available in the personal profile settings, we still want to walk through and understand the available settings and how they might be used. You need to focus on only one section, as shown in Figure 2.11.

To start, head over to your Facebook Page and click Edit Page. This takes you to the Page editor, where you can tweak a number of settings and adjust what appears in tabs, the permissions, and a number of other options to help you customize your

Page. We start in the Manage Permissions section, which is the main one we're concerned with here.

Figure 2.10   *Previewing what your profile looks like to specific friends or family.*

Figure 2.11   *Adjusting privacy or access options under Pages is controlled by two primary settings under the Page editor: Settings and Wall Settings.*

For the Settings option, you can choose the following:

- Can only admins see the page? Use this when building a page, but remember to deselect it when you're ready to go public!

- Restrict people from certain countries, which you can specify, from viewing the Page.

- Set age restrictions, thus preventing certain age groups from accessing the Page. These age restriction options are

  - Anyone (13+)

  - People over 17

  - People over 18

  - People over 19

  - People over 21

  - Alcohol related

- The next options that we need to consider are the Wall Settings options. These settings include some basic options for deciding which tab is the default landing tab, the default view of the Wall, and whether comments on stories can be expanded. Also, a set of fan permissions enables you to control fans' ability to post on the Wall, add photos and videos, and tag photos.

If you have trouble with spam, you can add a set of words that, when found in posts, get the post immediately tagged as spam. And you can choose a profanity filter that's medium or strong to block posts with offensive language.

Some brands limit the ability of fans to write or post content on their Walls. Although, in general, writing on the Wall shouldn't pose any issues, it is understandable that allowing anyone to post photos, videos, or links could cause a moderation issue. If you put the time into moderating and actively managing the Wall posts, you might as well leave it open to the community; however, if persistent issues with posted content occur, at least you know that the ability exists to limit one or all of these permissions.

Group Privacy Settings

The privacy settings available to Group admins are the same as those available to Page admins, except the way the options are laid out is slightly different. The one exception is that within Groups, you can control the visibility of the Group (as shown in Figure 2.12). Your options are

- **Open**—The Group is completely open. Everyone can see the group and join. It appears in search results and all its photos, discussions, and other content are visible to anyone viewing the group, even nonmembers.

- **Closed**—Everyone on Facebook can see the group and its members list, but only group members can see the content.

- **Secret**—The Group is completely hidden from all search results and does not appear in members' profiles. Nonmembers can't see anything about the group, or who's in it.

Figure 2.12   *Groups allow you to control the visibility of the entire Group to Facebook search results and to public search engines.*

It's important to know which way you want a Group to be, because after it has more than 250 members, you can't change the privacy settings. For all group types, members can add friends, but if someone finds a closed or secret group and requests to join, an admin must approve that person. You can also manually set an open group to require member approval by an admin.

As you can see, as Facebook has grown, it implemented many privacy settings to allow you to control how others can interact with you and your brand.

Facebook's Privacy Policy

As with any large social network, Facebook has developed, and continues to iterate, a set of policies that are the guiding rules of the network. The privacy policies and terms of services are put into place as a way to govern the large social network.

When Facebook originally started out, the network was private. Essentially all information was opt-in only. To view any information other than some basic data points and a bio picture, you had to be "friended" by the individual to see other information. But, over time, Facebook tweaked the platform and eventually moved toward a more open network. Information was still all opt-in, but these updates allowed users the option of whether they wanted to expose some, or all, of their information to Facebook Search results and external search engines. In a January 2010 interview, CEO and founder Mark Zuckerberg talked about the battle between openness and privacy. During a speech at the Crunchie awards, Zuckerberg stated:

> "People have really gotten comfortable not only sharing more information and different kinds, but more openly and with more people. That social norm is just something that has evolved over time...in the last 5 or 6 years, blogging has taken off in a huge way, and just all these different services that have people sharing all this information."

Although a lot of controversy occurred because of this speech, you shouldn't lose sight of what Zuckerberg and his executive team deal with at Facebook. Facebook, in terms of population, is one of the largest countries in the world. Therefore, Zuckerberg and his team need to implement strategies and policies that they think will be best for all the citizens of Facebook. Sometimes these aren't the popular decisions, but most of the time, they are done to help better the entire network. That will cause some percentage of people to become upset. This is the same thing that happens in any country when new laws are passed or existing laws are updated.

One example of trying to do the right thing for the entire community was during a major round of updates to the privacy policy during December 2009, when Facebook released a major update and change to its privacy policies. The goal was to give users more granular control over their privacy settings by, among other updates, allowing them to select, on a per-post basis, who can see content posted to their Facebook profile. Also, Facebook announced that it was removing regional networks. When Facebook was originally created, it included having to choose a network, such as a country, state, city, college, work, or other related groups. The concept behind this was that it would make it easier to connect with people in that group, and also that only those within the group could see your profile without being friends with you. This had the reverse effect when Facebook began growing at exponential rates. People became part of large networks, sometimes into the millions. This, of course, made privacy a moot point. So, in the December 2009 update, Facebook tried to change these issues. To help even further, Facebook provided a suggested privacy level for you that you could accept or tweak.

In an open letter to the entire network, Zuckerberg explained:

> "We're adding something that many of you have asked for—the ability to control who sees each individual piece of content you create or upload.... We've worked hard to build controls that we think will be better for you, but we also understand that everyone's needs are different. We'll suggest settings for you based on your current level of privacy...."

Immediately after this open letter was posted and the updates flowed in, revolt from the community started. The claim was that by creating these updates, although you could restrict your activities more, it actually tended to lead people to sharing more. Eventually, this calmed down, and people adapted to the new privacy policies and options.

Another controversial move in 2011 was Facebook's use of facial recognition technology to suggest tags in photos you've posted. That's right, Facebook might be able to figure out you're in one of your friend's' photos, and then suggest that the friend tag that person as you. You can change this when you click Customize Settings from the Privacy Settings page. Scroll down until you see Things Others Share (see Figure 2.13) and look for Suggest Photos of Me to Friends. Click Edit Settings.

Figure 2.13 *How to prevent Facebook from using facial recognition software to suggest that friends tag photos you might be in.*

Again, as with a large country, decisions are made and laws or guidelines are created that are put into place for the overall benefit or protection of the community. Not everyone will like these changes, and for some, it could, occasionally, restrict what they're doing.

Summary

Even though Facebook tries to ensure that you have the controls necessary to control your privacy, you should always be careful of the amount of information you share, not only on Facebook, but also on the Internet, in general. Although Facebook can provide many tools that can be beneficial to yourself and to your company, you should engage only at a level that you ultimately feel comfortable with.

3

Establishing a Corporate Presence

A corporation can develop a strong presence on Facebook in multiple ways. If you are an executive within a corporation, you might question why any company would want a presence on a social network that seems so personal in nature. If you don't want to fish in a pond that is packed with approximately 800,000 new fish every single day, then have fun somewhere else. We, of course, say that with some sarcasm. We do understand that some companies resist using Facebook for business purposes.

Personal or Professional?

Facebook was, for much of its history, seen as an exclusively *personal* social network. On Facebook you can let your hair down a little and interact with your college buddies, family, and close friends. You share pictures and videos from recent vacations or of your baby's first steps. You post your personal opinions on random topics, such as your favorite pizza toppings or who/what is annoying you today.

If you wanted to do any business networking, there was LinkedIn. On LinkedIn you can input your resume, get recommendations, and set up a group around your company, product, service, or industry and several other business-related activities.

The problem is that Facebook is growing at such a fast pace that you can't ignore it. And more and more professionals are networking via Facebook as well.

Some companies allow their employees Internet access to LinkedIn from work, but deny access to Facebook, Twitter, and other social networks.

You might be wondering why we're even talking about personal versus professional personas. Doesn't everyone keep their personal and professional lives separate? You're a different person on the weekends around your family and friends than you are when sitting across the boardroom from your boss, customers, or vendors. Right?

We understand the hesitation as to whether you should blend your personal and professional lives. Some people, the authors of this book included, have decided that everything we do is our life. We don't distinguish, for the most part, between a personal and professional life. Justin wants his business partners to know his personal interests in the Red Sox, Jay-Z, gadgets, and everything else that he's a fan of or has an interest in. People from both his personal and professional lives can see pictures from his wedding or his recent vacation. For him, it translates into a lot of business. Brian treats Facebook similarly.

People can establish a 360-degree view of who Justin is. They can get to know him as an individual before ever meeting at a networking event or having a conference call about a potential partnership.

With this approach, we can all interact on a personal level that might lead to a professional relationship. After all, at our professional core, we prefer to do business with friends. We trust our friends and hope that our friends trust us. We would never want to do anything to disappoint, endanger, or hurt our friends. Therefore, we tend to work harder when we do business with friends. It's usually more enjoyable and easier as well. Facebook provides the perfect opportunity to mesh friendships and business.

Generational differences also exist here. Generation X prefers less of a professional versus personal boundary than Boomers do, and Gen Y is even more social and open than Gen X. Judgments from one generation to another aside, these are important differences we need to understand when we market and network to different age groups.

This blending of personal and professional also helps to develop a strong community, real friends, and interesting conversations. Not everyone feels comfortable with or has the ability to meld their personal and professional lives. Even if you don't want to cross these two areas of your lifestyle with one another, and you prefer to keep Facebook personal and LinkedIn professional, you still should consider establishing a corporate presence.

Note that Facebook's guidelines suggest you do business mainly via Pages, not Profiles. If you've previously set up your business as a profile, you can now convert it into a Page. A warning before you do: Your friends will become fans, but none of your content will survive the transition—that includes all your photos, videos, and posts. Also, your vanity URL, or username, does not convert, and the old URL will no longer work.

Developing a Corporate Facebook Presence

Aside from the individual choice of whether to join Facebook and blend your personal and professional lives, consider establishing a presence on Facebook as a brand because it helps to *humanize* your brand. Facebook is a very personal social network. People like people, and in a social context, people like brands that are personal. Through the types of content that you choose to share on a Facebook Page or Group, you can show that your company is a lot more than a logo. You can peel back that logo to expose all the great personalities that make up your company.

Facebook is a thriving community sure to contain fans of your company, executives, product, or service. If you're shaking your head and yelling loudly that you don't have any fans, realize that your prospects, customers, and future fans are hanging out on Facebook. Developing a presence on Facebook gives you the opportunity to find these fans and activate them by providing them with a community in which they can interact with one another and with your company. You need to realize that the days of forcing your prospects, customers, and fans of your brand to go to a website of *your* choosing is gone. Sure, you can still drive traffic to your website and convert people through a contact or informational form. There is still a lot of value in corporate websites. But, nowadays, you have to go where your prospects, customers, and fans hang out and build communities with them there. This, in turn, can encourage them to visit your corporate website and engage with you on your turf. If you ignore that, you are missing valuable opportunities to develop a stronger community. For instance, if I hang out only on Facebook and you hang out only on Twitter, you're missing an opportunity to engage with me, even though I could be speaking your praises or running your name through the mud on Facebook.

With Facebook continuing to grow in popularity, it makes sense to develop a corporate presence. At the very least, establishing even a basic presence on Facebook can make it more difficult for others to claim your brand on Facebook—anyone could start a Page named after your brand and represent your brand in a way you wouldn't like. Because there are hundreds of millions of pages on Facebook, it can't effectively monitor all new pages. If you need more convincing about the importance of creating a Page, realize that Facebook is now the top driver of traffic, over Google, to large sites.

Getting Started

Now that we've convinced you to establish a corporate presence, how do you get started? What do you need to know? What about someone stealing your brand's name? Is that possible? What if someone says something bad about you on Facebook? Will that show up? What are *fans*? What's the ROI of our efforts? How much time do we need to spend to make it useful?

All these questions come up when corporations consider venturing onto Facebook. If any of those questions ran through your head, you're not alone. In fact, we bet that those questions are then followed by: "I don't want my employees on Facebook all day." "If they're on Facebook, how will I stop them from going on their personal pages, chatting with their friends, or checking out pictures from their friends' party last weekend?" "I can't afford to give my employees time to 'hang out' on Facebook. I need them working on their projects."

When a company is first created by a user, it is saved into Facebook's database so that when other employees join, they can find and use a standardized company name. This helps to link employees, and it allows users to search for you based on a company search. That means the first person who enters your company into Facebook needs to know how it should be listed.

This tip is helpful to find other employees, especially if you have a large organization or one that might be decentralized, with employees working from all over the world. This does not allow your employees, prospects or customers to socialize in a centralized area. To enable socialization, Facebook has created two different areas: Pages and Groups.

Facebook Pages

Facebook describes Pages as "a voice to any public figure or organization to join the conversation with Facebook users...a public profile lets users connect to what they care about." Facebook Pages are used by celebrities, bands, sports teams, corporations, films, nonprofits, and those users who have exceeded the friends limit on their personal profile pages.

When Facebook originally launched Fan Pages, it had limited features and looked different than regular profiles. However, as more people flocked to Fan Pages, Facebook changed Fan Pages to Pages and updated them so that they now resemble a regular profile. Pages allow the administrator to customize the tabs, add in basic information, and control whether fans can post on the wall, upload photos and videos, and other security controls. They also provide you with analytics (information and fans and posts) called Insights that are not available for personal profiles.

One of the biggest changes to the Pages occurred when Facebook created the Facebook Markup Language (FBML). Besides the other features of FBML, one of the ways that it can be used is to alter the look, feel, and behavior of Pages. You can now do this with iFrame technology. Some of the best examples of Pages are described in Chapter 10, "Best in Class Facebook Pages," on the Best in Class users, Pages, and Groups.

Getting Started with Your Facebook Page

Now that you've decided to create a Facebook Page for your company, similar to the setting up of your personal profile, you should take a number of steps to ensure that your Page is set up properly. The following are some tips to help you get started.

Create Your Facebook Page

The first step is to create and classify your Facebook Page. Start by clicking the Pages option in the left navigation of your Facebook home page. You might have to click More to find this option (see Figure 3.1). You can also reach this page by going to www.facebook.com/?sk=pages.

Figure 3.1   *Go to your Pages section by clicking Pages in the left navigation.*

This takes you to your Pages section (see Figure 3.2). After you've created Pages or have been made admin of Pages, you'll see of list of them here. This dashboard view tells you about notifications, total likes, and daily number of active fans.

From there, you can click the Create a Page button.

This takes you to the Create New Facebook Page section of the website (see Figure 3.3). Choose the best classification for your Page:

- Local Business or Place
- Company, Organization, or Institution
- Brand or Product
- Artist, Band, or Public Figure
- Entertainment
- Cause or Community

Figure 3.2   *Your Pages dashboard, with up-to-date information about each page.*

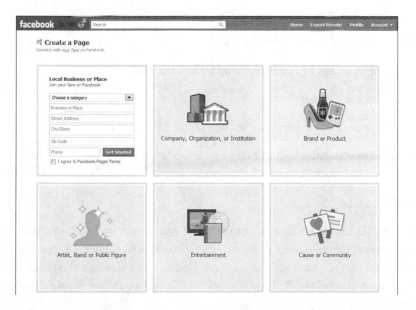

Figure 3.3   *The six main types of Facebook Pages. Here we've clicked Local Business or Place to show you an example of the type of extra information you'll be asked to enter before continuing.*

In every case, when you click, you'll have to enter more specific information. For example, the local business or place asks for address information.

Next, provide the name of your organization. Ensure that this is the name that you want to appear as your Facebook Page. You can't change the name after it's completed. Your only option will be to delete it and start over again (trust me, many businesses know this from experience). When you have carefully selected and typed in your name, you need to confirm that you have authorization to create the Page by providing an electronic signature.

You are now ready to start setting up your Page. You should spend time branding your Page, configuring all the options, and tweaking to your liking before telling the rest of the world about it. Put your best foot forward to start out and then continue to improve as time goes on.

Configure Settings

Again, similar to the personal profiles, Facebook allows you to configure a lot of settings (see Figure 3.4). Take some time to run through each of the sections and tweak to your liking. The first view of your new Page gives you six steps to complete:

1. Add an image.

2. Invite your friends from Facebook.

3. Tell your fans by importing contact information.

4. Post status updates.

5. Promote the page on your website with a Like box.

6. Set up your mobile phone so you can update the page from anywhere.

Upload Your Logo

Because this Page is set up as an extension of your brand on Facebook, you need to use your corporate logo (or your headshot if you're a solo entrepreneur, see Figure 3.5) as your default picture. This logo can be 200 pixels wide and 600 high. Select the thumbnail carefully. This thumbnail version will be shown beside all your status updates.

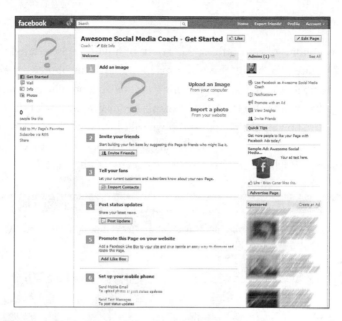

Figure 3.4   *This is a new page for a fictional Social Media Coach. Facebook guides you through six initial set-up steps. You can also see links for Insights and advertising to promote the page in the right-side navigation.*

Figure 3.5   *The Facebook Page for a motivational speaker. Note how the full 200x600 image gives his book some extra exposure, but the thumbnail is selected to focus on his face.*

Upload Photos

Do you have photos of your offices, your staff, or anything else related to your company? Create a couple of photo albums and upload the photos for everyone to see. Remember, not only are you trying to establish a presence on Facebook for your brand, but you're also trying to humanize your brand. One of the easiest ways to do this is by showing the people and physical office spaces that help your company to function on a daily basis (see Figure 3.6). Also, if your office space needs improvement, it might be good motivation to switch things up a little.

Figure 3.6 *The Marriott Napa Valley Hotel has nearly 500 photos to give you a better idea about what you're in for when you book with them.*

Additionally, if you have photos of your products, especially in action, or screenshots of your software, create an album for them as well. You can provide a short description of each photo or screenshot.

Upload Videos

Do you have client testimonials, product demos, behind-the-scenes videos of your operations, commercials, or interviews? Use the publisher on your Facebook Page to upload them (see Figure 3.7). Uploading videos takes longer than uploading photos. But it is another form of media that you can share with your prospects, customers, fans, and even employees. If you're not streaming all these videos already on your corporate website, your Facebook Page is a good place to bring together your videos from all across the Internet. Some pages don't automatically show the Videos option in their left navigation, so you might need to go to Edit Page, Apps, Edit Settings for Video, and then choose (add) next to Available (see Figure 3.8).

 Tip

Have you already uploaded your videos to YouTube? If so, you can install many YouTube applications on your Page. These applications pull in links to your YouTube videos. Many of them allow you to view the videos on your Facebook Page. None of them actually transfer the video file to the Videos section of your Facebook Page. There is nothing wrong with that, but we want to save you from hunting for hours for an application that does that. For new videos, from now on, you can use a service such as TubeMogul and push your videos out to many video services, including YouTube. TubeMogul can also load these videos onto your Facebook Page. That way, you serve your video up on many video platforms and extend their reach and the number of online communities that you share the video on.

Figure 3.7   *After you choose a file to upload, Facebook launches another window. When the file is uploaded, you can enter information about the video. After Facebook processes it, it will show up on your Page.*

Figure 3.8   *Making the Video tab visible in your Page's left navigation.*

Apps for Pages

Many of what were formerly Page tabs are now considered apps. Even the Photos and Videos links you see in your left navigation are considered apps. There are thousands more Facebook apps to choose from. Each different type of Page comes preloaded with a set of apps. For example, a band Page will come with a music player, video player, discography, reviews, tour dates, and discussion board.

Previously, there was an official apps directory, but Facebook shut this down. Now Facebook wants you to use the search feature to find apps. Figure 3.9 shows a search for apps that help you integrate your blog's RSS feed into Facebook. You can also do this with the Notes application, which we'll cover in a bit.

You can use many applications to help customize your Facebook Page, such as the following:

- If you own a restaurant, you could integrate OpenTable or Zagat Ratings.

- If you or someone else from your company does a lot of public speaking, you can upload your slide decks to Slideshare.net and then integrate their Facebook application onto your Page.

- If your company is active on Twitter, you can find applications that allow you to create a tab on your Page dedicated to your Twitter stream.

Figure 3.9 *A search revealing many RSS feed applications that can be integrated with your Facebook Page. Involver also has a good RSS app.*

Applications also exist for photo services such as Flickr, video services such as YouTube, polls such as Poll Daddy, calendar publishing apps, and thousands of other options that can help you to customize your Page.

Notes and Your Blog

While viewing your Page, click Edit Page, then click Apps, and you can add the Notes tab if you want to write notes or pull in your company's blog with its RSS feed. Under Notes, click Go to App, and then you'll see Edit Import Settings in the left navigation. Click that and you'll get Figure 3.10.

If your company doesn't have a blog, first consider taking steps to change that. Second, you can pull in any other RSS that your company might have, such as a Corporate News section on your website.

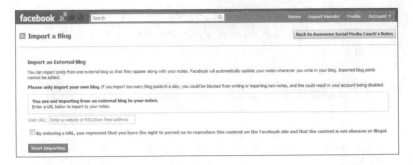

Figure 3.10 *Similar to the Notes tab on the personal profiles, Facebook Pages also allow you to activate a Notes tab that you can pull into your external RSS feed.*

After you've imported your RSS feed into Notes, you'll see what looks like your blog, but inside of Facebook's look and feel (see Figure 3.11).

Figure 3.11 *Here are some of Brian's blog posts from briancarteryeah.com pulled into a Facebook Page's Notes via RSS.*

Tip

Because the Notes feature in Facebook is limited in settings and features that you can control, you might also want to consider pulling in your RSS feed through one of the many available RSS applications. These RSS applications allow a more in-depth experience and interaction level with blog posts. These applications also give you more settings to control when and how your posts are pulled into the application and then displayed on Facebook.

Events

Set up the Events tab—If your company hosts events, puts on webinars, meetups, or any other online and offline event, you should create an event within Facebook to ensure that your Facebook Page is classified as the organizer (see Figure 3.12). This allows users on Facebook to register for the event and share it in their news streams to help extend the reach of the event. If you use an online event registration service such as Eventbrite (eventbrite.com, see Figure 3.13), it allows you to create a Facebook Event directly from Eventbrite so that you don't need to spend time duplicating the information.

Figure 3.12 *Mashable, a social media blog and one of the top-rated blogs in the world, uses the Events tab of its Facebook Page to show where it's holding meetups, parties, and other events around the country.*

Figure 3.13 *Eventbrite gives you step-by-step instructions for promoting an event from its site directly onto Facebook.*

FBML

Although all these Facebook applications enable you to customize the options and information on your Facebook Page, one application allows you to totally change the look and feel of your Facebook Page: the Facebook Static FBML application. FBML is best described by Wikipedia as

"...a variant-evolved subset of HTML with some elements removed.... It is the specification of how to encode content so that Facebook's servers can read and publish it, which is needed in the Facebook-specific feed so that Facebook's system can properly parse content and publish it as specified."

Essentially, that means that FBML is a simplified HTML coding language that enables you to mock up custom widgets or tabs on your Facebook Page (see Figure 3.14). This is beneficial to companies, celebrities, and public figures because it allows you to brand your Page with your specific colors, provide a similar layout to your other websites, and provide rich content on your Facebook Page.

The Reports of FBML's Death Are Greatly Exaggerated

In 2010, Facebook announced it would stop supporting FBML. In March 2011, it followed through. All this led to a lot of confusion and anxiety, but many were surprised to discover on July 8, 2011, that Static FBML was again the fastest growing Facebook application! It turns out there's a big difference between Facebook no longer *supporting* FBML (which means it won't do customer support for its issues), and the fact that you can still create with it and use it on Facebook. There are currently three apps in the top 30 most used Facebook apps that help you create FBML and HTML on Facebook.

- **Static HTML: iframe tabs:** http://apps.facebook.com/apps/application. php?id=190322544333196

- **Static FBML 3:** http://apps.facebook.com/apps/application. php?id=6009294086

- **iwipa: HTML + iframe + FBML:** http://www.facebook.com/iwipa

But if you want the absolutely easiest-to-use iframe app that will help you create a *reveal tab*, also called a *fan gate* (see Figure 3.14)—something that shows one image to nonfans and another image to people after they've clicked Like—check out Wildfire's free app at http://iframes.wildfireapp.com/.

If you're willing to pay a bit for advanced custom tab creation features, here are some of the players in that space:

- Lujure Assembly Line
- Involver
- Fan Page Engine
- North Social
- Pagemodo
- ShortStack

Check out how some of the Best in Class Facebook Pages discussed in Chapter 10 have utilized FBML and iframes. Several of these used Lujure for their custom tab creation. Then consider getting someone to do a little coding for you if you need something unique.

Figure 3.14   *This is how the Red Bull page appears before you Like it. You can see a faded out glimpse of what you'll get once you click Like. As soon as you do, the page refreshes to the post-Like view. Excuse me now while I go back and re-like my second-favorite beverage.*

The Discussions app—The Discussions app used to be standard on all Facebook Pages. But now, as Facebook Page managers have shifted to leading discussions by posting into fans' News Feeds, and with the advent of the much more active new Facebook Groups (since October 2010), it's probably not worth installing the Discussion app anymore. Most Page owners found it was difficult to get much activity there in the first place, because people didn't visit the tab much. Because people primarily experience Facebook through their News Feeds, you would have to constantly post about your Discussion area to get people to remember to go. This extra step is a waste of time. However, if you already have an active community in your Discussion area that's self-sustaining (see Figure 3.15), go on with yo' bad self!

Make your Page visible—Last, but not least, if you set your page so only admins could see it while you tweaked the settings and applications, and built custom tabs, make sure you go back to Edit Page, Manage Permissions, and deselect that box! Don't worry if it's not perfect. It's not meant to be perfect. If you waited to publish your Facebook Page, your corporate website, your blog, your product, or anything else until it is "perfect," you would never get around to publishing anything. You would be stuck in the cycle of forever tweaking, always finding something wrong that needs to be adjusted.

Figure 3.15   *The Discussions tab on the Ellen DeGeneres Show Facebook Page is still super active, despite all of Facebook's interface changes!*

What's Next

You've decided to start a Facebook Page for your business; you've spent some time customizing it; and you've published it. "Now what?" you might ask yourself. If you asked yourself that question, fantastic. If not, you should. Not even the biggest brands and most popular celebrities in the world are just suddenly found on Facebook because they've published their Page; unless of course, you're Justin Timberlake, Beyonce, or the new teen group of the year. That raises the question: "How do I get people to my Page?"

One of the first things you should do is to create an easy-to-remember URL that redirects to your Facebook Page. Facebook allows you to create a custom URL, sometimes called a "vanity URL," so that the URL is http://facebook.com/YourBrand. But you must have 25 fans first. Most people have their employees, friends, and family make up that first 25. While you're waiting to get to 25+ fans, you can either create a URL that is a subdomain of your website, such as http://facebook.mysite.com (which you set to redirect to the FB page), or you can use a

URL-shortening service and create a customized shortened URL, such as: http://bit.ly/brandfb. Whichever option you choose, make sure it's easy to remember because you'll never remember the default URL with its huge string of numbers like www.facebook.com/pages/Awesome-Social-Media-Coach/173403756065916. The next thing you should do is promote your Facebook Page. You can start in a number of ways.

Promoting Your Facebook Page

Email Signature

Adjust your email signature to include your Facebook Page, as shown in Figure 3.16. This is among the simplest tweaks you can make and will reach a lot of people, especially if you're someone who sends a lot of emails.

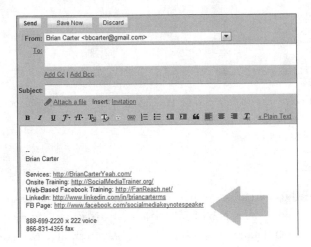

Figure 3.16 *Promoting your Facebook Page in your email signature. There are also services like WiseStamp that add a Facebook logo and hyperlink as well.*

Twitter

Begin promoting your Facebook Page on Twitter (see Figure 3.17). Don't spam your Twitter followers, but occasionally let them know, maybe a few times per week, that they can also connect with you on your Facebook. This helps drive more attention to your Page. Also, if they enjoy connecting more on Facebook than on Twitter, you will more likely have better, more in-depth conversations with them on your Page. You should also encourage any other employees or members of your team who also have Twitter accounts to begin promoting that you now have a Facebook Page. This is where having an easy-to-remember URL is very handy.

Figure 3.17   *A search showing how a number of businesses are promoting their Facebook Pages on Twitter.*

Facebook

Remember the six steps from Figure 3.4? Make sure you do all of those first. Similar to promoting via Twitter, you, your team, and your staff should use the Share feature on Facebook to occasionally share the Facebook Page into their news stream. This is easy to do but be careful not to do it too often. It is a source of annoyance to many users on Facebook because people "pimp" their Facebook Page a little too often. If you don't interact on your personal Wall often, you shouldn't share your Facebook Page on your Wall often.

Email Marketing

If your company sends out email marketing such as newsletters, company updates, or anything like that, you should have a call-to-action in every email campaign that encourages people to interact with you on your Facebook Page. When you first launch your Page, you might announce it in an article in your newsletter and encourage people to like it. After that, you should have that information in a static sidebar or in the signature section of your email creatives (see Figure 3.18).

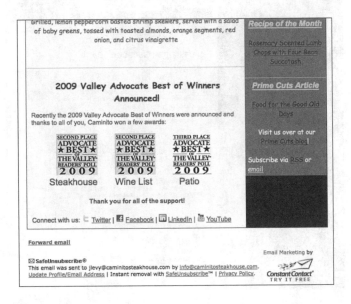

Figure 3.18   *An example of incorporating a Connect with Us section of your email newsletter in which you encourage your subscribers to connect with you via your Facebook Page (and other social networks).*

Company Website

Similar to your email marketing, you should show off the various social networks that you're active in, including your Facebook Page. You can do this by creating a separate tab and/or a sidebar widget on all the pages of your website where visitors can link to (see Figure 3.19).

Alternatively, if you want to call out your Facebook Page a little more, you can add a Like Box to your website. The Like Box can allow people to like your Facebook Page directly from your website or blog, see the other people that are fans of your Facebook Page, and interact with the Page (see Figure 3.20).

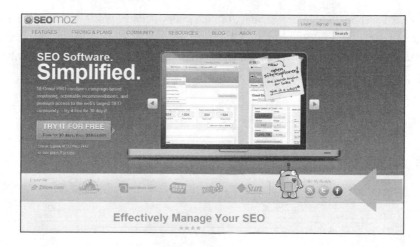

Figure 3.19   *Another easy way to encourage people to connect with you via your Facebook Page is to add linked social icons to your website. SEOmoz puts its social icons right next to the cartoon bot character it's made part of its branding, saying "Be My Buddy," thereby personalizing the brand.*

Figure 3.20   *Coca-Cola visibly promotes its Facebook Page by integrating the Like Box into its website.*

Facebook Ads

You can run targeted Facebook ads that appear in the right sidebar area of users' Facebook accounts with a message to encourage them to like your Page. We discuss Facebook ads in greater detail in Chapter 4, "Facebook Advertising: How and Why You Should Be Using It." But, suffice it to say that running a Facebook ad as a promotion of your Page is a cheap method to get your Page in front of a targeted group of Facebook users, as shown in Figure 3.21.

Figure 3.21   *Promote your Facebook Page by creating a targeted ad using the Facebook Ads system.*

Google AdWords

Just like buying a Facebook ad, you can attract fans for your Page by running Google AdWords. Include a call-to-action asking people to fan your Facebook Page. You might offer some type of special reward, contest, or something else to grab the person's attention. We haven't seen AdWords used often to promote Facebook Pages, and it doesn't make much sense when Facebook ad click costs are usually four times cheaper than AdWords clicks. Therefore, this option is not recommended.

Other Facebook Page Promotion Ideas

You can promote your Facebook Page in many other ways. You can also promote via commercials, radio spots, newspaper or magazine ads, or a number of other traditional forms of advertising. It all depends on what your company is doing for advertising, marketing, and engagement with your prospects and customers. At the end of the day, simply try to promote your Facebook Page wherever it makes sense within your advertising and marketing plans. You can do this in much the same manner as you would promote your website or other contact information. Some people laugh at grocery stores putting Facebook icons in one of their circulars—there's no way to click it and no URL—but it's still a great way to let people know your company is up to date, and some people will go home and search Facebook for it.

Facebook Groups

Whereas Pages are the public watering holes for fans of your brand, Facebook Groups are like private backroom parties. You can set up private communities for your company, both internally or externally. In October 2010, "new" Facebook Groups became a much more powerful marketing tool.

Facebook Pages are designed to provide companies, celebrities, or other public figures with the ability to establish a presence to allow them to interact publicly with their fans, prospects, or customers (see Figure 3.22). However, sometimes you want a private area in which you can engage a select group of customers or a special area just for your employees. This is where Facebook Groups come into play.

A Facebook Group can be best described as "a real-life interest or group or to declare an affiliation or association with people and things...you are creating a community of people and friends to promote, share and discuss relevant topics."

Review the privacy settings for Facebook Groups in Chapter 2, "Addressing Privacy Concerns."

These different levels of access can be beneficial when deciding why you want to set up your Group. If you're a smaller company and want to have a private area for your employees to engage, you might make the Group secret. However, if you're a large company and want to have an area for employees to hang out, you might set the level of access to closed so that you can decide who gets in.

Facebook Groups are usually created around a particular topic. But, as you can see, a Group can be used in a few unique ways and for corporate use, too.

In October 2009, Facebook transformed the format and functionality of Groups to be more similar to Pages. They now look and feel the same, including posting updates to your News Feed, thus leaving little differences between the two. The one major difference is that you can't install applications or extend functionality with FBML coding in Groups like you can with Pages. This limits the usefulness of Groups compared to Pages.

Figure 3.22   *Behind-the-scenes of a Facebook Group. Brian participates in five Facebook Groups daily. He finds them to be the best part of his Facebook experience.*

The "new" Groups in October 2010 meant several more major changes:

- Anytime someone posts or comments in the Group, everyone is notified via email or "red alert notification." That means you'll see numbers inside a red box above the clickable world icon in the upper-left corner of your Facebook screen.

- These emails can seem spammy to anyone new to the Group, so make sure you tell new members to turn off the email notifications if they don't want them (see Figure 3.23).

- There's also a chat feature now, specifically for chatting only with members of a Group.

- You can set up a Group email address so people can post via email while on the move. Note, though, that people with a Facebook mobile phone app can also access Groups directly through those apps. Emailed posts can be annoying because people often leave in their email signature and reply info from the previous email they received. After you set up a Group's email address, you can't remove it.

Figure 3.23   *To edit the Group notifications you receive as a member, click Edit Settings. You might want to turn off emails if you already visit Facebook several times a day.*

Set up options for Groups are limited. Choose a name and image for the Group. Select the privacy option you prefer. Write a description of the Group, and you're done! You might also want to create a Doc within the Group to explain policies.

Page or Group: Which One?

It is understandable that you might be a bit confused after reading this chapter and are trying to figure out how to properly brand your company on Facebook so that you can start engaging with your prospects, customers, employees, and fans. Both the Pages and Groups features within Facebook have many benefits. Which one should you choose and why?

Generally, if you're a brand, organization, celebrity, politician, or other public figure, and you want to engage with your prospects, customers, and fans, you want to set up a Facebook Page. Pages are public. That means that all features of the Page can be seen without having to become a fan of it. Everyone can join your Page and can promote it into their News Feed. Furthermore, the available features and level of customization is unparalleled when comparing it with the capabilities of Groups.

This isn't because Facebook has decided to neglect Groups. Facebook Pages are designed for brands, celebrities, and other public figures to be encouraged to set up public presences on the network. This is why in March 2009, Facebook made the decision to convert Pages into having a similar look, feel, and functionality of personal profiles. Facebook wants this to be another place for your brand besides your company website. For those who choose to embrace this, it can prove to be beneficial.

For all intents and purposes, a brand is equivalent to a person in Facebook. Also, because Pages are public, they're also visible to search engines.

Groups can be private, and you must request access to join a Group, unless a friend adds you first. Groups are great for focused discussions by the most passionate fans of a topic. A Group can also be a great solution for brands to create a private community if they lack funds to have an enterprise-level community developed. A Group is also good for companies that want a quick, private community for their team or a select group of customers. Although you should be careful about sharing sensitive data on Facebook because you don't control what happens with that information, it is an easy way to set up a private community quickly. You might start a Group that you invite select customers into for feedback purposes and for discussing an upcoming product or release, or you might allow direct access to particular individuals within your organization. If you choose to set up a Group for your employees, it is an easy way to communicate with them.

II

Intermediate Marketing Skills

4

Facebook Advertising: How and Why You Should Be Using It

You see them every time you log in to Facebook. You head over to your profile or check your Facebook Page or Group, and you're greeted in the right sidebar with advertisements. Ever wondered how they get there? How they always know some personal bits of information about you, such as your age or name? Or how your friends' names end up in some of the ads? Want to learn how you can put your own advertisement up? Welcome to Facebook Ads (see Figure 4.1).Facebook provides a huge number of tools, some of which you might not see fitting into your marketing campaign, but one of the easiest and most popular tools to integrate into your marketing campaign is Facebook Advertising.

Facebook has developed an advertising platform that is similar in many ways to Google AdWords, but possibly more powerful. If you're familiar with how the Google AdWords self-serve platform works, then Facebook Ads won't take long to learn. Where Facebook Ads differ from Google AdWords is that you can target your campaigns based on all the information that we discussed in the Introduction, "From Dorm Room to Boardroom: The Growth of Social Networks." Remember all that personal information you gave Facebook when you set up your account? You can use other people's info to target them for advertising. See Table 4.1 for a comparison of targeting options between the two ad networks. And you'll see in Figure 4.2 how they show in the right sidebar of Facebook's interface.

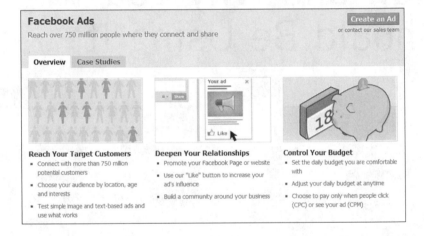

Figure 4.1   *The welcome screen at facebook.com/advertising explains some of Facebook Advertising's biggest benefits.*

Table 4.1   Comparison of AdWords' and Facebook Advertising's Targeting Capabilities

Target People With	Facebook Ads	AdWords Ads
Interests (Likes)	Yes	No
Intent (Search phrases)	No	Yes
Location	Yes	Yes
Age & Gender	Yes	No
Status	Yes	No
Workplace	Yes	No
Education	Yes	No

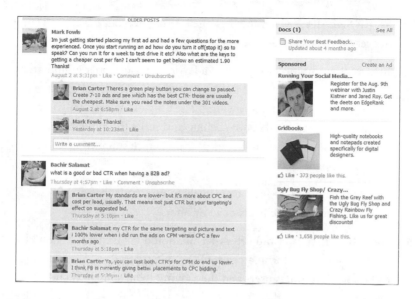

Figure 4.2 *Facebook Ads may or may not show depending on where you are in Facebook, but they're almost always in the right sidebar area.*

In this chapter, we talk about common reasons for rejections, a step-by-step guide to create an ad, how to measure your campaigns, and creative ways in which you can use the advertising platform.

Common Reasons for an Ad to Be Rejected

Before we walk through the steps you need to take to create a Facebook Ad, it is useful to consider the common reasons that your ad could be rejected. Make sure that you don't use any of these tactics, and your ad should pass with flying colors.

According to Facebook, the following are the 12 most common reasons for an ad to be rejected:

1. **Capitalization of every word**—Capitalizing every word can give you an unfair advantage over the ads that are running. Also, it is not proper grammar.

2. **Capitalization of entire words**—One of the easiest ways to scream "SPAM" to your target audience is with the capitalization of entire words. We've all seen these messages, and most of us are usually, if not always, turned off by messages such as LEARN HOW TO IMPROVE

YOUR SALARY. Even if the message is useful to you, the capitalization of every word makes it appear spammy.

3. **Incorrect grammar**—Do yourself a favor and use proper grammar. You and your company will not be viewed as professional if you're not using proper grammar and spelling. The only exception is if you purposely get clever with slang or spelling and it fits the audience you're targeting. Take time to proofread your ad before submitting it to Facebook for review.

4. **Inaccurate ad text**—Facebook is likely to reject ads that do not clearly state the company name, product, or offer.

5. **Deceptive discounts and offers**—This should fall under the "don't be dumb" rule, but unfortunately, some people try to deceive by making one offer that attracts users and then giving them something totally different when they click it. This will get your ad tossed by Facebook and could damage your online reputation.

6. **Irrelevant or inappropriate images**—Use images that are relevant to your ad. Also, make sure your images are clean. Similar to deceptive discounts, don't be dumb. Help to ensure Facebook is a safe and fun place for people to hang out. Facebook has cracked down on the use of irrelevant scantily clad women in ads, so it's likely those will be disapproved as well.

7. **Inappropriate targeting**—Why would you want to spend money targeting one group while speaking to another? Target those that you want your ad to reach—bottom line.

8. **Destination**—Facebook has developed some particular guidelines when it comes to where you can send your audience. Per Facebook: "All users must be sent to the same landing page when the ad is clicked. The destination may not include fake close behavior, pop-ups. Ads may only be directed to a website or iTunes. When linking to iTunes, the text must explicitly say so. Ads may not be directed to any other download such as PDF, PowerPoint, or Word documents."

9. **Sentence structure**—Be sure to use complete sentences. Proper grammar, spelling, and sentence structure will make your ad, and therefore your company, appear professional.

10. **Unacceptable language choice**—Language can't be degrading, derogatory, inappropriate, sexual, or profane in any nature.

11. **Incorrect punctuation**—Similar to other areas that we've talked about, this is yet another reason that your ad will make your company appear unprofessional. Ensure that someone proofreads your ads before sending them to Facebook for review.

12. **Symbols and numbers in place of words**—The sub-language of speaking in 140 characters (in text messaging and on Twitter) has changed how many people word a sentence. Instead of full words such as "for," many now replace it with the number "4" instead. This is cause for rejection by Facebook. Don't substitute symbols or numbers for words.

Step-by-Step Guide to Creating an Ad

One of the great things about Facebook Ads is that you can easily experiment with a few campaigns on Facebook. Because you can dictate exactly how much you want to spend, you can test whatever amount of money you feel comfortable experimenting with.

Now that you've decided that you want to experiment with running an ad, it's a simple process to create and publish your ad. It takes only four steps for your ad to appear for your target demographic.

1. **Design Your Ad**

   After you log in to Facebook, you can get to the advertising by either clicking the Advertising link at the bottom of your page (you might have to scroll twice if Facebook shows you more newsfeed posts) or by typing **http://facebook.com/advertising** into your browser address bar.

   From the advertising platform, choose the Create an Ad option to reach the ad editor. The first section is where you create your ad (see Figure 4.3). Select what the destination URL will be for the ad. It can be an external website or landing page, or you can choose to have your ad point to a Facebook Page, Group, or Application. Select the Title, Body Text (up to 135 characters), and upload an image, if you want.

Figure 4.3 *Design is the first of three tasks needed to create a Facebook Ad. As you add elements to your ad, you can preview the results right beside it.*

Depending on whether you use cost-per-impressions (CPM) or cost-per-click (CPC), you need to ensure that your ad is designed in a way that maximizes your advertising spending to achieve the goal of either pushing the user to a website or for brand awareness. How you design your Facebook Ad can greatly affect its success. In addition, you'll want to ensure that your ad is designed specifically for your target audience. The options available in Facebook Ads allow you to focus your attention on that target audience.

As you select the title and body text of your ad, be careful not to become too wordy. You don't have long to grab your audience's attention (Brian's general rule is that you have three to five seconds for the audience to get the point of your ad); therefore, make it targeted, simple, concise, and to the point. If your goal is to convince users to do something, such as click the ad to go to an internal or external link, you need to make sure you have a strong call to action and that your message directs them to complete that action, such as "Click here to register for the event."

Tip

When developing a call to action, make sure that you're direct: Tell your audience exactly what you want them to do. For example, tell them to click, like, or click and then enter their email address—whatever it is you want them to do.

Images are your direct shot into people's limbic system (the seat of the emotions). Images help grab the audience's attention and convey your message. You can't run an ad without an image, so make the most of it. Use your company logo, product shot, or other relevant image. Facebook Ad images are really small—the size limit is only 110 pixels wide by 80 pixels tall. (Hint: That's not very big.) Brian likes to say that faces are often the best ad images because...we're on a website called FACEbook! And human beings are hard-wired to look at faces for threats or validation.

If you want to create an ad that displays one of your Facebook Page's posts, choose Sponsored Page Post under Story Type (see Figure 4.4), and then you can select which of your recent posts you'd like to use, or just allow the ad to display the most recent post. If you choose the latter, the ad will update automatically (and go through the approval process) each time you create a new post on your page.

 Tip

Consider using a landing page: When you convince users to stop what they're doing and take time to interact with you online, make sure that you direct them to the most relevant landing page. That can be an internal Facebook page such as a Group, Page, or App. If you point your audience to an external website, consider creating a specific landing page for your Facebook Ad.

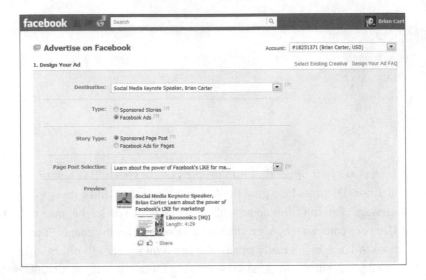

Figure 4.4   *If you select a sponsored page post, you can turn any recent post into an advertisement.*

2.   **Target Your Audience**

Decide *who* you want to target with your ad. Facebook allows you to target based on 11 different filters, such as location, age, birthday, sex, keywords, education, and so on (see Figure 4.5).

As you go through these different filters, make sure that you spend quality time thinking about who you want to target and how the filters can assist in limiting your ad to that specific audience. This is one of the best features within the Facebook Ad platform as compared with Google AdWords. Make sure that you take advantage of this feature and apply the proper filters. For example, if you only serve customers in the Northeast, make sure you apply those filters. Don't just leave the location open to everyone in the United States.

Figure 4.6 covers the rest of the ad targeting options, including interests, advanced demographics, education, and workplaces.

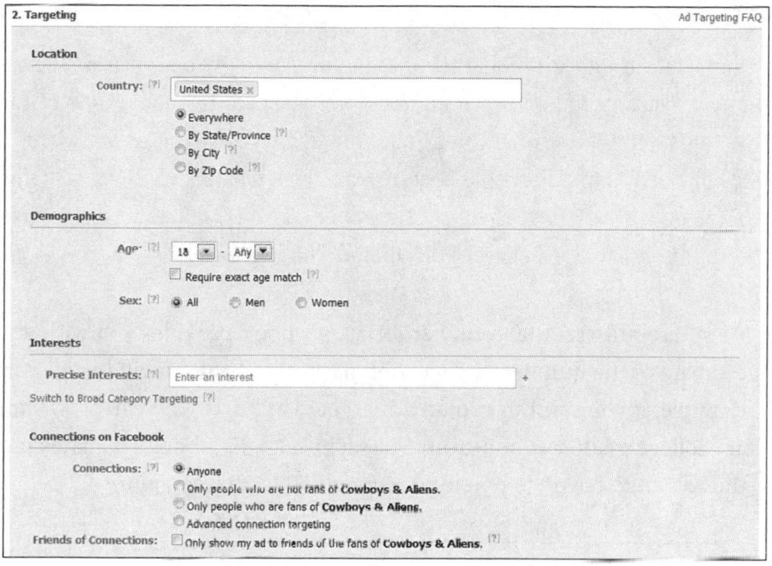

Figure 4.5   *Facebook advertising has so many options, they won't all fit on one page. Here is the first group. As you design your ad, be sure to spend some time considering these targets.*

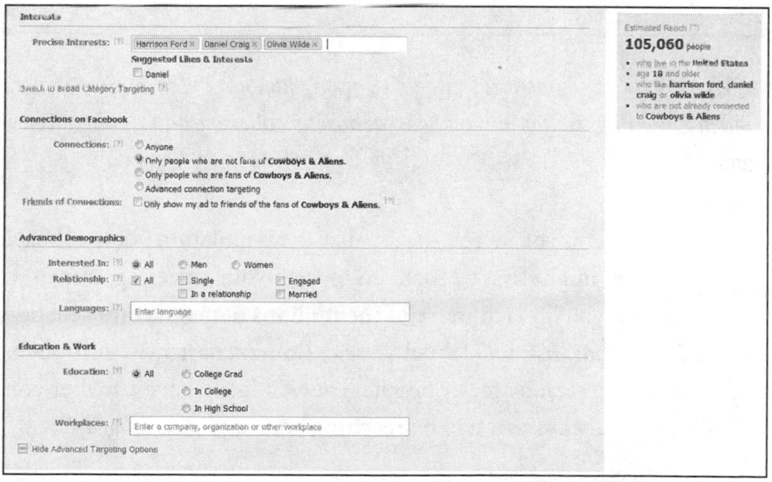

Figure 4.6   *Here are the rest of the ad targeting options. While setting your targets, you can view the estimated audience that your ad will have the potential to reach.*

Tip

Using "precise interest" targeting can be an extremely powerful way to
narrow the size of the potential audience for your ad. Because some of the
other targeting options might not limit your search as much as you want or
need, this can help narrow the search. Facebook also allows topic targeting
(topic targets are distinguished by a number sign) if you need to expand a
precise interest to a wider, yet still related, audience.

As you set different targeting criteria, Facebook provides you with an
estimate of the number of Facebook users that your ad will reach. For
example, if you want to run an ad targeted at 22- to 27-year-olds who
are college graduates and from Massachusetts, Facebook estimates that
the ad would have the potential to reach 509,420 (see Figure 4.7).

Figure 4.7 *You can segment ad targets by many factors. Here, Facebook shows you
could reach more than half a million Massachusetts college graduates between the ages
of 22 and 27.*

The more criteria you select, the smaller the population you will reach.
Although you might first be inclined to keep your targeting more
broad so that you'll reach more of the millions of people on Facebook,
don't follow that instinct. Target your customers narrowly. Although
your ad will be seen by fewer people, you will likely have a higher conversion rate because you will be reaching your target demographic.

A potential problem with targeting is that it is based on the fields that
you and others choose to fill in. Therefore, if you don't disclose your
location, or if you have moved without updating your location, the
ad estimation tool may be off. Facebook has become very clever with
finding user locations, though. Even when you don't disclose where
you live, Facebook uses the IP location of where you normally use the

Internet to guess at your location—and it serves ads based on that. Brian doesn't have his city listed in his Facebook profile, but he's traveled to San Francisco or New York, and while using the hotel's Internet connection, been served ads targeted to people in those cities.

3. **Create a Campaign and Set Pricing**

   After you create your ad and decide who you want to target, the next thing you need to do is to create the actual campaign and set your pricing.

   Facebook provides you with the option to set a daily budget and to determine whether you want the ad to run continuously or if you want to target the ad only between certain dates and times (see Figure 4.8). This can be incredibly useful, depending on the reason for running the ad. While deciding how much you want to spend daily and what period of time you want the ad to run, you need to choose what you want to pay for.

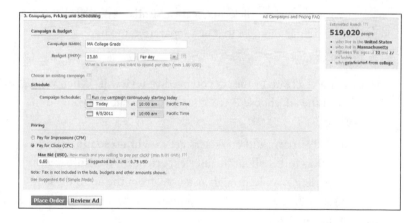

Figure 4.8 *Decide what your daily budget is, the schedule for your ad, and whether you want to pay for impressions (CPM) or clicks (CPC).*

   Facebook allows you to choose between paying per thousand impressions of the ad (CPM) or paying per click on the ad (CPC), as shown in Figure 4.7. Because both options rely on what others are bidding for the same targets, you need to set what your maximum bid is. Facebook provides a suggested bid range based on the other bids it currently has. If you don't bid the minimum, Facebook will warn you that your ad might not be shown. In these types of pay-per-click auctions, the bid is just the price of entry. Your actual cost per click will be higher when targets have higher suggested bids.

If you try to push users to either an internal or external website, and the success will be based on conversions, you probably want to select CPC. You pay per click; therefore, you pay only for each time people actually click through. It is then your job to set up that internal or external landing page properly to grab their attention and convert them, based on what your definition of conversion is.

If you want Facebook Ads to help with branding and awareness and don't want as many clicks, you can use CPM because what you actually care about is getting your ad in front of as many people as possible. Keep in mind, however, that Facebook makes money on clicks, so ads that don't get clicks will stop showing sooner.

Whichever option you select, CPC or CPM, be sure to test with both to see how each converts for you. The way to do that is to create a CPC version in one campaign, click on Create a Similar Ad, switch the new ad to CPM bidding, and save that in a separate campaign.

4. **Review and Submit**

   Now that you've created your ad, you need to review it. When you're satisfied with the ad, choose Place Your Order to submit your ad to Facebook.

   Many times advertisers and marketers get caught up so much in the process that they forget about the user experience. To ensure a positive user experience, walk through as a user, from the ad to the landing page. Ask colleagues, friends, or spouses to take a run through the steps, and then gather their opinions.

   After you submit your ad to Facebook, it goes through a quality review to ensure that the ad fits Facebook's quality guidelines. Upon approval of your ad, it will be published according to the targeting and pricing options you selected while creating your ad.

   Facebook provides robust analytics about the performance of your campaigns. Use these analytics. Don't ignore them. Dive in and evaluate how your campaign is performing. Rip apart the analytics to gain knowledge, and then make necessary changes to ensure that the money you spend is put to its best use.

Analyzing Performance

Facebook provides an excellent reporting tool to gauge the performance of your ad campaign. Analyzing performance is important so that you can make adjustments, not only after your campaign but also during the campaign. By monitoring your performance in real time, or near real time, you can make immediate changes that can turn the tides of a lagging campaign that's only draining your bank account.

When you head into a specific campaign, you're immediately greeted with a dashboard (see Figure 4.9) where you get an immediate glance at your campaign's performance. From here you can edit your campaign, its status, the daily budget, or duration. You can also see a roll-up report of the major key performance indicators of your campaign in Figure 4.10, including the following:

- **Status**—Active, Paused, or Deleted
- **Reach**—Unique number of people who saw the ad in this time frame
- **Frequency**—Average number of times each person saw the ad
- **Social Reach**—Number of people who saw that one of their friends had already liked what you were advertising (or RSVP'd to your event or installed your app)
- **Connections**—Number of people who liked your page, RSVP'd, or installed your app
- **Clicks**—Number of clicks received, which includes likes, RSVPs, and app installs
- **CTR % (click-through rate)**—Clicks divided by impressions (you can see impressions if you click Full Report)
- **Bid**—The bid you chose
- **Price**—Average amount you're paying (CPC or CPM)

You can see this immediate information for all campaigns you might be running or have run in the past.

If you're bidding CPM, you might have trouble figuring out what your cost per click is. Just click Full Report and you'll see both your CPM and CPC for each ad (see Figure 4.11). This is the actual cost. It might be confusing and irrelevant to see CPM cost when you're bidding CPC, but it's enlightening to see CPC cost when you're bidding CPM. You also get to see the total spend per ad in that time period. And seeing impressions can help you discover whether one of your ads isn't showing enough.

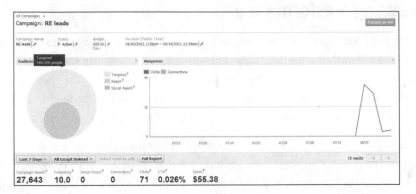

Figure 4.9 *Facebook graphically demonstrates that I've targeted 180,720 people (lighter circle), and my ads have shown to 27,643 of them in the past seven days.*

	Campaign Reach	Frequency	Social Reach	Connections	Clicks	CTR	Spent
	27,643	10.0	0	0	71	0.026%	$55.38

Name	Status	Reach	Freq.	Social Reach	Connections	Clicks	CTR	Bid	Price
MV_CID=3477&MVAL=1_1_1_1	▶ ▾	3,648	2.2	0	0	1	0.019%	$1.00 CPC	$0.75 CPC
MV_CID=3477&MVAL=1_1_2_2	▶ ▾	7,593	4.0	0	0	8	0.026%	$1.00 CPC	$0.74 CPC
MV_CID=3477&MVAL=2_2_1_1	▶ ▾	719	5.9	0	0	1	0.024%	$1.00 CPC	$0.00 CPC
MV_CID=3477&MVAL=2_2_2_2	▶ ▾	375	3.6	0	0	0	0.000%	$1.00 CPC	$0.00 CPC
MV_CID=3477&MVAL=2_2_1_1	▶ ▾	6,091	2.3	0	0	4	0.028%	$1.00 CPC	$0.86 CPC
MV_CID=3477&MVAL=3_3_2_1	▶ ▾	8,583	5.0	0	0	13	0.030%	$1.00 CPC	$0.70 CPC
MV_CID=3477&MVAL=3_3_1_1	▶ ▾	379	3.6	0	0	0	0.000%	$1.00 CPC	$0.00 CPC
MV_CID=3477&MVAL=4_1_1_3	▶ ▾	387	3.5	0	0	0	0.000%	$1.00 CPC	$0.00 CPC
MV_CID=3477&MVAL=4_2_1_1	▶ ▾	6,454	2.7	0	0	4	0.023%	$1.00 CPC	$0.95 CPC
MV_CID=3477&MVAL=4_2_1_2	▶ ▾	11,031	7.7	0	0	21	0.027%	$1.00 CPC	$0.77 CPC
MV_CID=3477&MVAL=5_1_1_3	▶ ▾	374	3.5	0	0	0	0.000%	$1.00 CPC	$0.00 CPC
MV_CID=3477&MVAL=5_1_2_1	▶ ▾	1,748	2.2	0	0	1	0.026%	$1.00 CPC	$0.83 CPC
MV_CID=3477&MVAL=5_1_1_2	▶ ▾	4,285	2.4	0	0	2	0.019%	$1.00 CPC	$0.92 CPC
MV_CID=3477&MVAL=6_1_1_2	▶ ▾	8,119	3.9	0	0	8	0.025%	$1.00 CPC	$0.79 CPC
MV_CID=3477&MVAL=6_1_2_3	▶ ▾	693	6.1	0	0	1	0.024%	$1.00 CPC	$0.92 CPC

Figure 4.10 *You can run many different reports to dig into your campaigns. This enables you to identify trends on the fly and make adjustments.*

 Note

You probably noticed the weird ad names in Figures 4.10 and 4.11. Those ads were created by a Facebook multivariate ad testing tool called Optim.al. Brian has found that using this tool lowers his average ad CPC by at least 15%. He believes a part of that performance improvement is simply being forced to test more images, headlines, and ad copy. The more things you test, the more likely you are to find the best performing ads.

277,744 Impressions   **71** Clicks   **0** Connections   **0.026%** CTR   **$55.38** Spent   **$0.20** CPM   **$0.78** CPC

Date Range	Campaign	Ad Name	Impressions	Clicks	CTR	CPC	CPM	Spent
07/31/2011-08/06/2011	RE leads	MV_CID=3477&MVAL=3_2_1_1_3	1,350	0	0.000%	0	0	0.00
07/31/2011-08/06/2011	RE leads	MV_CID=3477&MVAL=2_2_1_3_1	14,120	4	0.028%	0.86	0.24	3.44
07/31/2011-08/06/2011	RE leads	MV_CID=3477&MVAL=1_1_2_2_2	30,005	8	0.026%	0.74	0.19	5.94
07/31/2011-08/06/2011	RE leads	MV_CID=3477&MVAL=3_1_1_2_1	0	0	0.000%	0	0	0.00
07/31/2011-08/06/2011	RE leads	MV_CID=3477&MVAL=5_2_1_1_2	10,282	2	0.019%	0.92	0.18	1.94
07/31/2011-08/06/2011	RE leads	MV_CID=3477&MVAL=4_1_1_3_3	1,351	0	0.000%	0	0	0.00
07/31/2011-08/06/2011	RE leads	MV_CID=3477&MVAL=6_2_1_2_1	21,561	5	0.023%	0.84	0.19	4.20
07/31/2011-08/06/2011	RE leads	MV_CID=3477&MVAL=2_1_2_2_3	1,355	0	0.000%	0	0	0.00
07/31/2011-08/06/2011	RE leads	MV_CID=3477&MVAL=2_1_1_1_2	0	0	0.000%	0	0	0.00
07/31/2011-08/06/2011	RE leads	MV_CID=3477&MVAL=1_1_3_1_1	6,847	1	0.015%	0.75	0.11	0.75
07/31/2011-08/06/2011	RE leads	MV_CID=3477&MVAL=5_1_2_3_1	3,888	1	0.026%	0.63	0.21	0.83
07/31/2011-08/06/2011	RE leads	MV_CID=3477&MVAL=6_1_2_1_3	4,208	1	0.024%	0.92	0.22	0.92
07/31/2011-08/06/2011	RE leads	MV_CID=3477&MVAL=3_1_2_3_2	42,715	13	0.030%	0.70	0.21	9.14
07/31/2011-08/06/2011	RE leads	MV_CID=3477&MVAL=4_2_1_2_2	84,681	23	0.027%	0.77	0.21	17.62
07/31/2011-08/06/2011	RE leads	MV_CID=3477&MVAL=6_1_1_3_2	31,915	8	0.025%	0.78	0.20	6.25
07/31/2011-08/06/2011	RE leads	MV_CID=3477&MVAL=5_1_1_2_3	1,326	0	0.000%	0	0	0.00
07/31/2011-08/06/2011	RE leads	MV_CID=3477&MVAL=4_1_2_1_1	17,325	4	0.023%	0.95	0.22	3.79
07/31/2011-08/06/2011	RE leads	MV_CID=3477&MVAL=1_2_1_2_3	4,215	1	0.024%	0.66	0.16	0.66

Figure 4.11   *The full report shows impressions, actual cost per click, and spend per ad.*

Additionally, Facebook provides three campaign reports:

- **Advertising Performance**—This report shows the same types of data you see on the dashboard, but you can control the reporting parameters better, as well as export the data to Excel or a CSV file.

- **Responder Demographics**—This report provides demographic data, thus allowing you to see who is clicking on your ads. This allows you to adjust targets or optimize text, or to understand who is attracted to your ads. Again, this information can be filtered by reporting parameters and exported.

- **Conversions by Impression Time**—This report shows the number of conversions organized by the impression time of the Facebook Ad a conversion is attributed to, categorized by the length of time between a user's view or click on the ad, and the conversion (that is, 0-24 hours, 1-7 days, 8-28 days). This report (see Figure 4.12) helps you see whether your fan growth campaigns are getting more fans from the ad itself (like_page_inline) or from people going to the Facebook Page (like_page) and when.

Through the use of the three reports that Facebook provides and the main dashboard, you can measure and adjust your campaigns on the fly, thus making better use of the money that you invest and allowing you to hit your target audiences in a more effective manner.

Date ?	Tag Name	Campaign ?	SKU	Conversions ?	Post-Imp (0 to 24 hours)	Post-Imp (1 to 7 days)	Post-Imp (8 to 28 days)	Post-Click (0 to 24 hours)	Post-Click (1 to 7 days)	Post-Click (8 to 28 days)
Jun 2011	Black's	blacksphotography smilinggirl	like_page	149	2	6	2	133	4	2
Jun 2011	Black's	blacksphotography smilingguy	like_page	321	17	6	2	289	6	1
Jun 2011	Black's	blacksphotography smilinggirl	like_page_inline	1,359	1	11	0	1,347	0	0
Jun 2011	Black's	blacksphotography smilingguy	like_page_inline	1,861	13	16	0	1,832	0	0

View Advertising Report   Export Report (.csv)   Generate Another Report   Schedule this Report

Report Type: Conversions by Impression Time   Summarize By: Campaign   Time Summary: Monthly   Filter: blacksphotography smilinggirl blacksphotography smilingguy   Date Range: 6/1/2011 – 8/3/2011

Figure 4.12 *In this Conversions by Impression Time Report for an advertising campaign for Black's Photo Corporation, you can see that many more fans came from likes on the ad than from likes on the Facebook Page. Also, almost all the likes happened within 24 hours—very few were delayed.*

Summary

It might seem easy to understand why or how you want to use Facebook Ads as part of your marketing campaign; however, you can use Facebook Ads in several ways. Let's review a few of them:

- Product launches
- Webinars
- Recruitment
- Branding/awareness
- Event marketing
- Social good campaigns

Although each uses the same basic elements, they can have different impacts depending on your goal. If several of these concepts fit with your company, you should experiment with them to see which seem to resonate with your target audience. As you can see, there are many uses for Facebook Ads that can integrate into your current online marketing strategy.

Similar to other features around Facebook, the advertising platform will continue to evolve with new features and improved analytics. Until then, use this as a guide to navigate the Facebook Ads platform and begin experimenting. Try CPC versus CPM, A/B test ads with the same targets, adjusting target audiences, and monitoring all your activity.

When used properly, Facebook Ads can be a powerful tool, and provides a significant advantage to any company that uses it.

Facebook Page Analytics: Tracking Your Success

How effective are your Facebook marketing and communication activities? How many of your fans are seeing your posts? Which posts get more engagement, and why? What can you do to improve your results? Facebook offers a wealth of statistics and insights into the performance of your Page and posts. By reviewing these, you can learn what your fans respond to and don't, what's keeping you from getting more responses, and how to improve. Internet marketers have found over the past decade that using analytics is essential to success, and Facebook marketing is no exception.

Quantify and Improve Your Page's Performance

Internet marketing, which includes social media, search marketing, email marketing, and more, is a diverse profession. Depending on your background, you may or may not have been exposed to the idea of web analytics. Analytics is the discipline that seeks to quantify and graph performance. It's essential to any marketing system if you want to get better results and remain competitive in an ever-evolving marketplace. Even if all you want to do is socialize with your fans, insights from analytics will help you calibrate your messaging, topics, and approach to better interest and engage your audience.

The first metrics you'll see as a Facebook Page administrator are impressions and feedback rate. These will show on each of your posts right above the post date and time (see Figure 5.1). This data won't show right away—it can be delayed up to 24 hours. Impressions are the number of times your post has been displayed to users. Feedback rate is the total number of likes and comments divided by impressions.

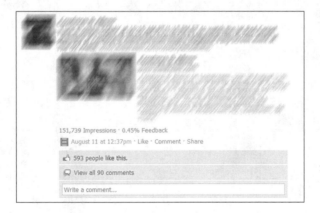

Figure 5.1   *Page administrators are able to see how many impressions (displays or views) each post got and the feedback rate (likes plus comments, divided by impressions).*

Inside Facebook Page Insights

If you have a Facebook Page, you have access to some pretty in-depth analytics called Insights. Go to your Page, and then look in the right-most column for the View Insights link (see Figure 5.2). Clicking it takes you into the Facebook Insights.

Figure 5.2   *As an administrator, you have additional options available in your right-most navigation. Click View Insights to see your Facebook Page analytics.*

The first thing you'll see is your Page Overview (see Figure 5.3). This page shows an overview of your User and Interaction information. For some strange reason, Facebook Insights shows a lot of the interaction information under the Users category, and not very much under Interactions.

Figure 5.3   *The Facebook Page Insights overview.*

Initially, what you see in the overview is for the most recent 30 days, but you can customize the date range if you want.

- **New Likes** is the number of people who've liked your Page (become fans) in that time period. There's also an up or down arrow showing a percentage change compared to the previous time period. Lifetime Likes is your total number of likes, all time.

- **Monthly Active Users** is how many Facebook users have interacted with your Page's post content or viewed the Page, and this includes nonfans. This metric also shows a percentage trend compared to the last time period.

Active Users is further broken down by time periods in the first chart. It makes sense that fewer people view or interact with your Page on a specific day than over the period of a week or a month.

In the Interactions section, you get even more metrics:

- **Post Views** is the number of times your posts have been seen in News Feeds. Fans will see multiple posts, so this number is much higher than your fan count.

- **Post Feedback** is the number of likes and comments on your News Feed stories. This is less than the Monthly Active Users because it doesn't include Page views.

Let's go deeper and take a look at more data and charts by clicking the Users option in the left navigation (under Page Overview).

The Users Section of Facebook Page Insights

There are six more charts and a lot more metrics on the Users page. Note, as you read this, if you see what you think may be inconsistencies, the sample charts in this book are from several different Facebook Pages.

Active Users—This chart is the same as the one on the Overview Page.

Daily Active Users Breakdown (see Figure 5.4)—This chart shows interactions with posts for each day. It's a good idea to deselect the Post Viewers box because that number is often much bigger than the others and doesn't allow you to see variation among the other metrics.

In this example, post likes are more common than post comments, and that's typical of most Pages. It's also common to have more likes than unique Page views. Your fans will see posts in their News Feed much more often than they go to your actual Page. This sample Page gets a higher than average proportion of Page views.

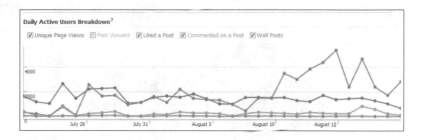

Figure 5.4   *The Daily Active Users Breakdown.*

New Likes and Like Sources (see Figure 5.5)—This chart shows how many new people liked your Page each day. This chart displays the typical weekly arc that's common to most web analytics—people behave differently on different days, but in a consistent way each week.

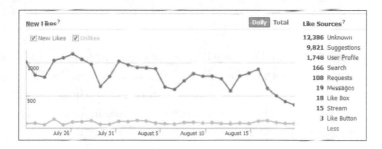

Figure 5.5   *New Likes and Like Sources.*

When you see a decline in new likes, as in this example, you might want to consider new and more aggressive promotional tactics, such as Facebook advertising.

Next to the New Likes chart you'll see a list of the top sources of these fans. Facebook can't always track all the sources, so some are unknown.

Demographics (see Figure 5.6)—There are two parts to the demographics insights Facebook Page Insights gives you—the age and gender chart and the lists below it.

You can use the age and gender chart in a number of ways. For example, ask if this demographic fits other data you have about your target audience. If not, either you might need to more actively target other demos with Facebook ads, or it could be your other information sources are inaccurate. Because Facebook has a huge amount of information given voluntarily by users, chances are this demographic information is highly accurate. If anything, older groups might be underrepresented when people above a certain age misrepresent their age, or refuse to enter it.

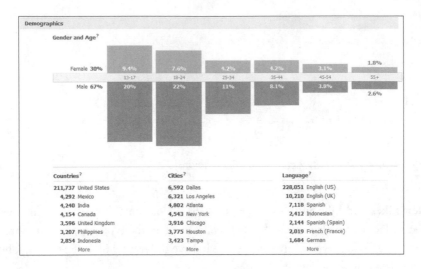

Figure 5.6 *Page demographics, including gender, age, location, and languages spoken.*

The Countries, Cities, and Language lists can be expanded to show more, but unfortunately you cannot see all countries, cities, or languages. You might want to compare the number of fans you have in various cities to their total populations to arrive at penetration figures. Are there cities you need to focus on more? Create some ads focused on people in those cities to even out your penetration.

Page Views (see Figure 5.7)—This chart shows how many people actually visit your Facebook Page. In a PageLever study on this topic (published on AllFacebook. com), only one to six percent of fans visit your Facebook Page on a daily basis. The rest see your posts through their News Feeds.

Below the chart, you can see which part of your Page users visited, including your page's Wall and other tabs. The typically low number of Page visitors and even fewer visits to custom tabs is why Brian recommends advertising and posting (to fan News Feeds) as your main Facebook marketing strategies. Custom tabs are nice, but have limited impact.

Figure 5.7 also shows external referrers, which are visits that originate from outside Facebook. In this case, the top external referrer was the company's website. Search engines are another big referral source. If you send people to your Facebook Page from your marketing emails, you might also see webmail domains and subdomains in this list.

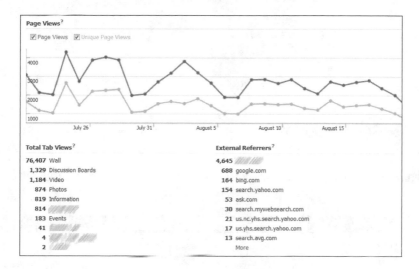

Figure 5.7   *Views of your actual Facebook Page and tabs, along with other websites that send traffic to your Page.*

Media Consumption (see Figure 5.8)—This chart compares your fans' consumption of photos, videos, and audio. After you post videos, photos, or audio, when people click them, it is tracked here. This can be useful if you're wondering how effective your post types are.

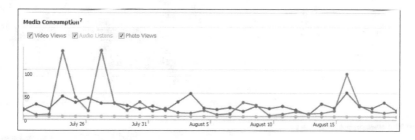

Figure 5.8   *Views of your actual Facebook Page, not News Feed.*

The Interactions Section of Facebook Page Insights

If we switch over to the Interactions subsection, the first chart, Daily Story Feedback (see Figure 5.9), is similar to its counterpart on the Overview Page, but this one also includes Unsubscribes. An Unsubscribe is not when viewers unlike the page, but instead they click the down arrow on your page's posts in their News Feed and choose to Hide your posts (see Figure 5.10).

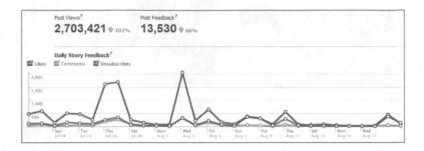

Figure 5.9 *Daily Story Feedback shows daily Likes, Comments, and Unsubscribes.*

Figure 5.10 *In your News Feed, you can hide all posts from a friend or page without unfriending or unliking. This is called an unsubscribe.*

In this case (see Figure 5.11), if you see more unsubscribes than comments, and most of your posts' Feedback rates are below 0.5%, there's a good chance your posts aren't resonating with your fans.

Brian recommends you try to get a 1.0% Feedback rate on your posts. Feedback rate is indicative of how interesting fans found the posts that they saw. Even if you're not currently reaching a high percentage of your fans (impressions divided by fan count), you can still achieve a 1.0% or higher Feedback rate with interesting posts and calls to action, such as "Click Like if..." or "Tell us in the comments below..."

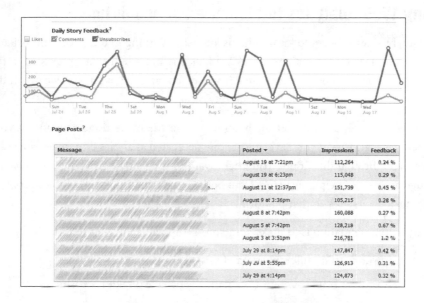

Figure 5.11   *Here, likes are deselected in the Daily Story Feedback to better show the relationship between comments and unsubscribes. In the Page Posts section, Insights shows your previous 10 page posts, how many times they were seen, and their Feedback rate.*

Advanced Facebook Page Insights

If you want even more insights about your Page than Facebook delivers, we recommend you try the paid third-party service PageLever. Using its insights, you can discover the following:

- What's the optimum frequency with which to post to your particular fans?

- Are the demographics of your active users different from your overall fan base?

- Which types of posts and content get you the best Feedback rates?

- What's the best time of day to post to your fans?

- Which source of fans leads people to unlike the most?

The answers to these questions are different for each Page and audience.

Using Web Analytics to Measure Facebook Impact

Many businesses want to know what is and isn't working in terms of actions Facebook fans take on the main website. Are fans buying? Are they as interested in the website content as people who come from search engines? What can we do on the website to get more Facebook fans to buy or take some other goal action?

The way you set up your web analytics to answer these questions depends on your analytics platform. If you have at least one dedicated analytics employee, they can help you through this. If not, you might want to use Google Analytics, because a huge amount of help is available from both Google and independent bloggers for doing-it-yourself with that platform.

Our recommendation is to make sure your setup will allow you to test:

- How fans from different types of posts behave on your website
- How users from different Facebook ads behave on your website

Armed with that information, you can adjust your tactics to get more of the results you want on your website.

6

Using Facebook to Develop Communities

Facebook contains hundreds of thousands of communities. People form communities around their interests, hobbies, events, companies, products, services, celebrities, schools—even their favorite foods! We create and participate in these online communities the same way we do in the real world. We engage with one another, bond, share articles, upload photos and videos, and invite others with similar interests to join. At the same time, advanced community platforms are taking the place of some old-style forums. Some companies choose to build these independent communities with services such as Jive and Lithium. These enterprise-level communities offer expanded features and more customization, but they're also expensive and more suited for larger companies and organizations. Also, because these premium communities are set up on a different domain or a subdomain of your website, you have to work harder to bring people to the party.

Facebook, on the other hand, helps you build community quickly and affordably. Facebook is an ocean where community builders can fish for people with similar interests or hobbies.

As discussed in Chapter 3, "Establishing a Corporate Presence," you need to decide between a Page and a Group when figuring out what features will be needed for your community or what your specific preferences are. We recommend starting with a Page and adding on Groups as needed. No matter what your choice, you can quickly and easily set up a community on Facebook.

Another benefit of using Facebook to set up communities is that it offers greater reach by breaking down geographic walls. Some traditional communities do grow large enough to break into local chapters and community groups all over the world. With Facebook it's not necessary to separate into localized communities, unless users decide they want to. Instead, they can all interact and benefit from one another, regardless of their location.

As you build your community, you need to decide who will be your community manager. Ideally, this person should be either you or someone from your team. As the community manager, you need to give your community reasons to keep coming back. All of us today have too many things competing for our attention. Those that get our attention and are interesting, helpful, useful, or otherwise needed will stay top of mind. Therefore, to continue to grow an active and growing community on Facebook, you need to engage your community; however, you can't just engage them by simply updating your Page or Group status every day. You need to provide content in various formats because all members of your community will demand to receive their information and content in different ways. Some of us prefer video, whereas others love photos, and some might want links to thought-provoking content.

Let's explore some of the different types of communities that can be formed on Facebook, how users are utilizing them, and along the way, some tips to help you maximize engagement within your community. In this chapter, we'll discuss several types of communities:

- Customer communities built around companies, products, and services
- Corporate communities for private internal discussion
- Personal communities for networking and business

In the remainder of the chapter, we'll talk about how to grow membership and interaction within Facebook communities.

Building a Community for Your Company, Product, or Service

More and more of your prospects and customers are on Facebook; therefore, you should not ignore Facebook as a viable way to form a community. Even if you have created an enterprise-level private community, you should still ensure that your brand is properly represented on Facebook. Facebook might even be a source of new community members for your private community, whether through a Facebook Page, Facebook Ads, or both.

You can use Facebook to create a Page (see Figure 6.1) or Group around your company, product, or service. This serves as your main presence on Facebook and as another outpost from which you can communicate and connect with your prospects, customers, or fans.

Figure 6.1   *Coca-Cola's Facebook Page. People from all over the world post here many times per hour.*

Developing an active community around your company, product, or service on Facebook can be beneficial, especially if you are successful at encouraging conversations. Why is engagement so powerful on Facebook? First, every time a community member likes or comments on one of your posts, Facebook can notify the member's friends and is more likely to show that interaction in other fans' News

Feeds. When you generate consistent interaction, you keep your brand top of mind with prospects, customers, and fans. Couple that with regular ads and the addition of new content within Facebook and other areas around the Internet, and you've strengthened and magnified your brand.

Some companies use both a Facebook Page and a Group—sometimes multiple Groups! For example, one veterinary supply company has a Page with more than 44,000 fans (see Figure 6.2), and a separate Group that serves all its customers and potential customers who own Rottweilers (see Figure 6.3). This group has more than 800 members who have created more than 6,000 posts.

Figure 6.2 *VetDepot has 44,000 fans and features one fan's pet each week in its Page's main photo.*

Do Pages or Groups Create More Community?

We covered the differences between Page and Groups in Chapter 3. If you recall, Pages provide more marketing and analytics options, whereas Groups provide more notification and privacy options. Neither really creates more community, per se, but here is what each is really good at:

- **Pages**—People rarely go back to the actual Page after becoming fans. Fans will see your Page posts, but not other fans posting on the Page.

Fans will stop seeing your posts if they don't like them or comment. As a result, you must lead and stimulate discussion. Ask for comments and likes.

- **Groups**—Everyone in a Group is notified when another Group member posts or comments, so people go back often. You don't need to do as much to keep people engaged. The members help you keep people interested. People who don't want this much activity will leave the Group, so they will probably never be as big in membership as Pages. Thus, these are great for subgroups of your customers who are extremely enthusiastic about specific topics.

Figure 6.3 *VetDepot's Rottweiler owner page receives more than 100 posts and comments per day.*

How Does Community Build ROI?

Sometimes in-depth discussions of community or engagement bring up latent questions about social media ROI. The best way to answer this is that building community does the following:

- Increases awareness of your brand through friends of fans
- Increases fans' and customers' trust in your brand

- Increases customer loyalty to your brand
- Decreases customer acquisition costs

All these things can increase your company's profits.

Building Private Corporate Communities

Facebook provides the opportunity for you to use Groups to form private communities. This is great for companies that might have distributed workers or a growing workforce and wants to have a common area for its team to hang out and engage with one another. Large corporations tend to have private enterprise-level communities built for them using a professional community platform. But companies that don't need a lot of features, or might not have budget for an expensive platform, can turn to Facebook to fill that communications void.

Many corporations have realized that their employees are all on Facebook and already spend a lot of time interacting on the platform. So, instead of forcing them to log in to yet another website, they decide to use Facebook as an internal communications platform for their community.

One of the downsides to using Facebook instead of a private community is that although the Group can be private, you don't control the data. Therefore, be cautious when sharing anything private or proprietary. You don't control the data and are not privy to decisions that Facebook might make concerning the platform, and you wouldn't want to wake up one day to find out that—although this is unlikely—Facebook decided to make Groups completely public, thus disclosing confidential data that could be detrimental to your company and a benefit to your competition. If you have those needs, you're best suited to contact one of the many private enterprise-level community platforms or a private network like Yammer.

Using Facebook as a Focus Group

Continuing with the concept of using Facebook as a private community for your company, what about creating a Facebook Group to be a private focus group for your company, product, or service?

You could invite specific prospects or customers to this Facebook Group and use it as a platform to

- Provide demos and exclusive access
- Show off pictures of upcoming products or software releases
- Ask for candid feedback

You might not want to show anything you're worried about leaking out. However, if you're engaged in any type of blogger or PR relations, that is a risk you always run when showing early releases of a product or software version—and leaks aren't always bad, are they? Sometimes they feed the buzz and increase customer anticipation the same way a new movie trailer does.

Building Personal Networking Communities

Facebook offers us the ability to build our own personal communities. These communities are built around us and not a hobby, interest, or other subject where we are the community manager. Most of the time these personal communities form on the user's personal profile; however, when these communities grow to be large, the user needs to create a Page to avoid hitting friending limitations set by Facebook. Either way, these communities can grow to be larger and more powerful than a traditional organization at times. How is this possible? The social web allows us to become, as Chris Brogan and Julien Smith coined, "trust agents." Brogan and Smith define trust agents as

> "[D]igital savvy people who use the Web to humanize businesses using transparency, honesty, and genuine relationships. As a result, they wield enough online influence to build up or bring down a business's reputation.... In an online world defined by transparency, becoming a trust agent is no easy task, but once you've established your reputation, you can build influence, share it, and reap the benefits of it for your business. When you've learned a trust agent's secrets, your words carry more power and more weight than any PR firm or big corporate marketing department."

Many of the tips that have been provided here and throughout the rest of this book can be useful for personal profiles as well. As you build your corporate online brand, it is important to also build your online personal brand.

How can you develop a strong business network around your personality?

Be Helpful

One of the easiest ways to begin building a strong community is to be as helpful as possible, as often as possible. Be a resource for your community. By providing help to your community on a regular basis, they can begin coming to you with questions. Your community can also begin to recommend you to others because of your resourcefulness, and that can allow your community to continue to grow larger and tighter.

Connect Often

Connect often with the greater community. You can do this by commenting on other users' statuses or sending a private message if you know someone is having a rough day. Make sure you note people's birthdays and use that as an easy way to connect with them on their special day. Go through other users' pictures and videos and leave comments. If you realize that you haven't reached out to someone in a while, make sure you stop by and say hi.

You'd be surprised how much impact you can have on the larger community by just being there and connecting. This can become even truer as your personal community begins developing into a larger community. People will notice that you're connecting often both with your community and the larger community that is Facebook.

Be a Connector

While you're busy connecting often with the members of your community, be a connector as well. Are there two people who you think could mutually benefit by connecting? Send them a message introducing them. As Chris Brogan has described to me many times in the past, you want to be at the "elbow of every deal." By playing that elbow role, you're being helpful and connecting with members of your community. At the same time, you're building up equity because those people that you connect with will remember you forming that connection for them. That doesn't mean that they owe you a favor, per se. But you'll find that the more often you try to be helpful by being considered a connector, the more goodwill and similar situations will come your way.

Use Lists

Using the List feature within Facebook can help you to create small communities for yourself based on interests, location, school, work, or anything else you want to create a list around (see Figure 6.4). Although this won't help to build a community in the sense that you invite people into a private area where you connect, it can help you to connect often with members of your personal community. By setting up Lists and checking in with those Lists often, it can help to make a growing personal community more manageable. It can also help you to organize your personal community around the many different segments of your life.

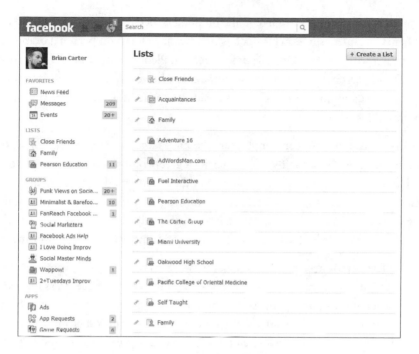

Figure 6.4   *Make use of the Lists feature for helping to categorize your friends. Suggestions for lists include by school, work, interest, or geographic location.*

This can help you to segment your sharing of information, especially if you have a wide range of tastes. For instance, you might be a foodie, and therefore you like to share recipes, interesting articles, discuss TV food shows, and leave status updates about the different restaurants you visit. You might decide that this information wouldn't be of interest to people you work with. By adding those members of your community who are foodies, you'll ensure that you're sharing that content only with them. For your foodie community, they will appreciate the targeted information, even if they don't realize that you have created a foodie list. (Currently, people in your list are not notified that you've put them in a list.)

Although all these suggestions can help you to grow a community, develop relationships, build influence and reputation, you need to ensure that everything you're doing is genuine. Please don't be fake in trying to grow a community. Don't do it for the numbers or for the perceived power that you might develop. It ruins people's trust and doesn't bode as a positive strategy for you personally or professionally—or for your company.

How Corporations Benefit from Employees' Personal Social Networks

Although it might not seem like it, the building of personal communities can also be beneficial for business. This book is not meant to focus on personal branding. That's not why you're taking the time to read it. Plenty of other books address the benefits of personal branding using online tools; however, it does matter to touch on it for just a moment as it relates to businesses benefiting from large personal communities.

Businesses can benefit from employees who have large personal communities on Facebook. How? Because if you're fostering a great company culture where your employees enjoy where they work and what they work on, they're more likely to want to share interesting projects they're working on, product releases, or other company news. If they have formed a large community on Facebook or any other social network, they're likely to turn to that community to share that information.

With a few keystrokes, influential social networkers can at times create more conversations about the news and more traffic to your website than a press release could. Even if on a pure numbers basis it does not send more traffic, it can be more targeted traffic and conversations. If your employee informs other influencers, that piece of content can get shared through several degrees of separation. Your employees have built up trust with their community and by being human and sharing what matters to them—in this case, their work—your employees are also helping to humanize your business.

Having employees that have a strong personal community can sometimes be more powerful than a company presence on Facebook. Remember, people prefer to connect with people. Therefore, it makes sense to foster and encourage employee engagement on Facebook. Of course, you first want to have a discussion to create a social media policy to let employees know what you consider appropriate and to ensure they know what about the company they should not make public.

Building a Community Around a Hobby or Interest

For both customer communities and personal networks, you can sometimes be more effective by building the community around a hobby or special interest. These niche communities have been around for years. Many of us have spent time on a forum board doing research or engaging in a topic that was of interest to us.

These topics can range from a love for vehicles, music, exercise, a city, or just about anything else you can think of (see Figure 6.5). People tend to belong to multiple groups in their personal and professional lives; therefore, online communities serve as great areas for them to stay engaged with others.

Figure 6.5   *Wine Searcher's current Page, the biggest private brand of its kind on Facebook.*

An example of highly engaged communities based around an interest or hobby are the wine communities formed on Facebook. There is no shortage of Pages dedicated to the celebration and discussion of wine.

One in particular definitely serves as an object lesson for others to follow, in more ways than one. As shown in Figure 6.6, the Wine Page (www.facebook.com/pages/Wine/20410752104) was originally created by Wine Searcher (www.wine-searcher.com, the largest and most used independent search engine for wine). Instead of creating a community around Wine Searcher, its team decided to create the community around the greater topic of wine. As of November 2009, the Facebook Page had more than 750,000 fans. Any given status update had hundreds of likes and comments.

Figure 6.6 *Wine Searcher's original Wine Page, which was reclaimed by Facebook.*

Unfortunately for Wine Searcher, Facebook made a change to its policies—the name of the page was too general (Facebook believed people were liking Wine itself, not the Wine Searcher company, and that this was potentially confusing for or deceptive to users). After September 2009, the fans of Wine were no longer in Wine Searcher's control, and Wine Searcher had to move to a new Facebook Page. At this time, it has about 90,000 fans, and it is still ahead of Wine Spectator and Wine Library TV in sheer fan count.

As with the development of personal communities, it might seem odd that I've mentioned forming a community around an interest or hobby in a book that is geared toward businesses and, specifically, marketers. But for every interest or hobby, there are plenty of businesses that support that interest. If you're a foodie, you might visit or be involved in restaurants, food television shows, kitchen gadget stores, and cooking classes. Does your business support or provide products and services for one of these activities? If so, you could involve yourself with other communities already created on Facebook, or you could create your own Page or Group to build a community. Instead of creating it around your product or service, it could be created around the hobby or interest that your company, product, or service provides. This community wouldn't be used to solely promote your company, product, or service, but would be used instead to have conversations around the specific industry that your company is involved in.

Brian has built several Facebook Groups around his personal interests, and some of the relationships gained in these Groups have led to business opportunities. In fact, Brian came to the work of revising this book through relationships formed in a Facebook Group. When he creates a new Group around a specific interest, he uses Facebook ads to seed in a few hundred members and then lets the Group grow organically.

Building Community Membership with Facebook Ads

Although huge brands might already have millions of fans and might not need to use Facebook ads, small and medium-sized businesses might have trouble growing a community of the size they want. Although in the earlier days of Facebook you could get a lot of free fans easily (as the Wine Page did), now it's harder to do so. Facebook has eliminated some of the functionality that made free fan growth possible, and Page owners are more sensitive to what they see as spam promoting other Pages and Groups. Facebook ads fill this gap and can be used to build a sizable fan base or group in an affordable way.

Why Pages with Millions of Fans Still Might Need Ads

There is one reason even Pages with millions of fans might want to start a new Group or Page: invisibility to existing fans. Facebook's EdgeRank algorithm determines which fans see your Page's posts.

Over time, fans that haven't liked or commented on posts no longer see posts from your community page. One study found that posts with pages with more than a million fans were seen daily by only 2.79% of their fans. That means they didn't really have a reach of millions, they had a reach of just tens of thousands. The upshot is that fans and members give you a chance to keep people interested, and if you fail in that task, you lose them. Brian calls these fans that can't see you anymore zombies. You can run sponsored story ads to show recent posts to them in hopes of reanimating them, but those can be expensive. Another option is to start a new Page or Group on a topic related to your brand, get these people back, and this time, keep them interested.

How to Get Affordable Fans and Group Members

There are two main ways to target potential community members with
Facebook Ads:

- Use the targeting criteria on the Facebook ad-creation page
- Target with the headline and ad copy

The cheapest clicks usually come from targeting no-brainer precise interests. For
example, if your business sells cooking-related items, target cooking or the name of
a popular cooking show. You can always refine with demographics when you better understand your audience.

But if you can't get these targeted ads cheaper than $1.00 per click, leave the tar-
geting wide open and call out to the audience in your headline. For example, you
might target everyone in the United States and use a headline that asks, "Do you
love cooking?" Only your potential fans will click this, and because the targeting is
so wide, the competition is low, and the cost per click will stay low as well.

 Note

> If you're looking for Page fans, make sure the Destination is your page and
> that the ad preview shows a Like button. When people click Like on the ad,
> they become a Page fan without even visiting the page! Without this Like
> button, your fans will be much more expensive because you introduce the
> extra step of going to the Page first. About 75% of these folks waver and
> might not click Like on the Page itself.

How to Build Interaction Within Your Community

Providing consistent and diversified content can become harder and harder as you
go along. When you first set up your community on Facebook, you'll think of all
kinds of information to share. But as time goes on, you might find yourself strug-
gling to provide a consistent flow of information. Here are a few suggestions to
help you continue to engage with your community and provide a consistent flow
of content.

Just remember, the purpose of content is to create conversation. You know those
crazy coffee table items they call "conversation pieces"? We're trying to find

interesting, unique, funny, thought-provoking content to put on Facebook so people can socialize around it.

Upload Photos

Do you have product or software photographs or screenshots that you can share? Create albums for each of your products or different sections of your software and upload your photos and screenshots (see Figure 6.7).

Figure 6.7   *VW uploads photos of its various vehicles. It also allows fans of the Page to upload photos.*

Other ideas include the following:

- Upload photos of your team at work.
- Create a photo tour of your office.
- Take photos of events you sponsor, speak at, or participate in.

If you want, you can upload the photos one at a time, commenting on each, asking for likes and comments. Each photo is a potential conversation piece, so you might not want to upload them all at once.

Upload Videos

You can use the video functionality within Facebook to provide content. Most people like TV and movies, and we're accustomed to it, so this is a powerful medium to use. Video allows your community to create a bond with you because they can connect with a human face. Compared to the written word, a podcast, or a photo, videos show life in motion.

If you have a product or software, try creating a short demo, or series of demos, showcasing a specific feature. Other ideas include the following:

- Upload customer testimonials.
- Develop a list of frequently asked questions and answer one per video. Then you can point people to that video when they have a question. If there are a lot of questions, maybe you could organize them into categories and create multiple videos. In the description for the video, you might include a link where the viewer could go to read the text version of the answer.
- Create a list of your industry's jargon and terms, and define one per video.
- Record interviews with people from your industry and upload those interviews. Link the video to a full-text version of the interview elsewhere.
- Shoot quick snippets from your team and create a video thanking your customers for their business.

Tagging back into creating a community based on interests, look at how Red Bull benefits from videos (see Figure 6.8) because of its strategic marketing decision to associate its brand with extreme sports.

Ask Questions

One of the easiest and most basic ways to trigger people to interact with you, especially on Facebook, is to simply ask a question (see Figure 6.9). Because the status update will drop into the live news feed, it is easy for others to quickly leave an answer. As more people continue to engage, the status update will keep floating back to the top of the stream. If you jump in and start interacting as well, you'll create a nice discussion based around something as simple as a status update.

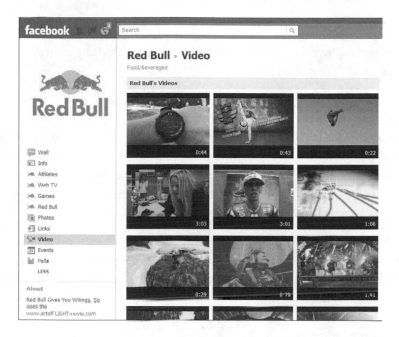

Figure 6.8 *Red Bull brands itself by partnering with extreme sports athletes and events. This lends itself to exciting video topics it can share on Facebook.*

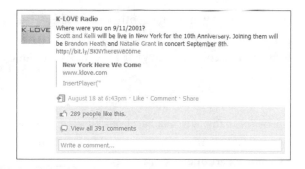

Figure 6.9 *K-Love, a national radio network, asks a question of its fans.*

So, what kind of questions are you supposed to ask? Ask anything. Ask your community how they're doing today. Pose a question with a link to an article in your industry. Ask for feedback on something you're working on. Whatever the question is, make sure it is about your community and not you. Make them feel like they're part of the community. For more insight on what to ask about, read the following sections.

Sell the Dream

Afraid that you're talking about yourself too much? Not getting enough engagement?

Brian came up with a concept that can help companies get their fans talking even in the most difficult cases. He calls it "Selling the Dream." You probably already know what the benefits of your product or service are. But have you thought about what dream you're helping your customers fulfill? What will their life or business look like with the benefits you give them? Try to outline that dream, and see whether it's different for your various types of customers (many companies have already researched and modeled several customer personas).

Now, start asking questions and posting photos and videos that make them think more about that dream. Connect this with how you'll help them reach that dream. Even the most boring product or service can be connected to people's emotions with this technique.

Provide Exclusives

Is there something that you could share with your community on Facebook that isn't shared anywhere else yet?

This is especially important if you interact with some of these same people in other online communities such as Twitter, MySpace, LinkedIn, or a private social network. By sharing unique content with your Facebook community, they will be encouraged to return often.

If you have a medium-to-strong community, try first announcing a new product, a software release, or company news via Facebook. If your community figures out that you're likely to release company information via Facebook, it will continually check in and be an active part of the community.

Instead of always porting in your YouTube videos, or uploading videos that you have also uploaded to other video services, how about creating some videos directly within Facebook?

Upload some new product designs and share them on Facebook exclusively first. Maybe leave them up there for a week or so before you then also upload them to other photo services.

Ask Them What They Want

These are a few ways that you could create various pieces of content to keep your community engaged. The most important aspect of keeping your community engaged around your company, product, or service is to figure out what your community wants and needs to get from spending its precious time on your Facebook Page or Group. This could be the dream you're selling. Then provide the community that level of engagement and type of content repeatedly and consistently.

Check in with your community regularly to see whether you're providing what they want. When you do decide to experiment, measure success by tracking the engagement. Look at the feedback rate and impressions for each post. Are they going up? If so, you're getting more engagement and visibility.

Nurturing Your Community

Now that you have decided which type of community you want to build, either a Facebook Page, Group, or both, and you've spent some time tweaking the settings and building up your community, you need to continue to nurture it. What should you do? Just post some status updates from time to time? That seems kind of lame, doesn't it? This seems to be one of the top questions received by companies after they set up a Facebook Page or Group. It's understandable. On the surface, when you set everything up, besides keeping things tidy and updated, it can seem difficult to see how you might nurture and continue to strengthen your community. Take a few of the following thoughts into consideration.

Run Contests or Sweepstakes

A sure-fire way to get engagement by your community is to run contests or sweepstakes that are available only to your Facebook community. The simplest and fastest way to do this is by encouraging responses to a particular question or discussion topic. You can offer a free month of service, a discount on your online store, and more. Note that Facebook's terms require you run contests via an application, and Wildfire is the best known such platform.

Simply Engage

One of the easiest steps you can take is to engage your Facebook community. Don't just spend all this time creating this fantastic community and then leave it to rely on only receiving automatic updates from pumped in RSS feeds, YouTube, or Flickr applications. Come hang out in your community. Update your status once or twice a day. Use a status update to ask your community how their day is going or their thoughts on a question. Make a few comments back to some of the people who have taken the time out of their busy day to engage with you. Again, this sounds simple, but it is so often overlooked and neglected. Just being there puts you far ahead of a lot of other companies, possibly even your competition.

These are just a few of the many ideas that you can use to help keep your community engaged. Communities, generally, don't manage themselves. They need someone around to keep prodding them through engagement, stimulating conversations, and various forms of content. The more often you can do that with your community, the more of a nurtured, vibrant, active community you will have on Facebook. This becomes even more important if you decide to set up a Facebook Page instead of a Group because all this engagement will be public to everyone, not just the members of your community.

As we start talking about all this engagement, I can sense some hesitation starting to build up. I know exactly what you're worried about. You're worried that someone will post something negative on your Wall about you. You're worried that you will be mocked, ridiculed, or hated on for one reason or another. You want to know how you can control for that.

How Do You Know Whether You're Doing a Good Job?

Brian likes to tell people to set the bar at 1.0% Feedback rate. With Facebook's changes to the News Feed in late 2011—where sometimes fewer people see posts, but only the ones who like your posts the most—it might be realistic to expect Feedback rates above 5.0%. There's more discussion of that in Chapter 5, "Facebook Page Analytics: Tracking Your Success." But you can eyeball any Facebook Page, even if you're not an admin, to see how good it's doing with visibility of posts and interaction:

1. Look at 5 to 10 of the Page's posts.

2. Count how many likes and comments on each, and do a rough average of the total.

3. Is this number about 1/100 (1.0%) of the fan count? If so, it's doing incredibly well.

On the other hand, if you look at Coca-Cola's Page, it has 33 million fans but only around 10,000 likes and comments per post (see Figure 6.10). That's only three-tenths of a percent of its fan base.

Figure 6.10 *Despite having 33 million fans, Coke is getting only 10,000 or so likes and comments on each post. Is that good enough?*

That means Coke is probably visible to a fraction of those 33 million fans. We've seen huge pages like that still get 0.1%–0.3% feedback rates, which means Coke is probably visible to only between 1 million and 5 million fans. That's still a lot of people, but not nearly as much as you would have thought when you saw the 33 million number. And the takeaway is that if a competing page with 10 million fans does a better job at engagement, it might be visible to more Facebook users than Coke is. The only way to win with EdgeRank is to get more likes and comments on every post.

You might have the sense by now that this engagement can be time-consuming! Even a small business needs to devote at least 15 minutes a day to it. And the bigger your community or social media ambitions, the more it could turn into a full-time staffer. In Fortune 500 companies, there might be an entire social media department.

Should You Police Your Community?

The issue of negative comments is one that every brand who signs up for a Facebook Page has to deal with. Although this could be an issue for Groups, especially those with controversial topics, you might be more concerned about Facebook Pages because the comments and content are always public. But keep in mind that because few people go back to the actual Pages, and because fans don't receive Pages posts from other fans in their News Feeds, only the biggest brands are really vulnerable here. On smaller Pages, it's possible that none of your fans will notice a negative Wall post, or at least very few will, and not right away.

For bigger pages and for any sized Groups, however, people will see the negative post. If you're a big company with the hundreds of millions of users, some people have probably had a bad experience with your company. Although in an ideal world only positive information would be talked about publicly by others, this certainly is not the case. Many corporations, when I meet with them for the first time, are leery of hearing what people are saying about them. What you don't know can't hurt you. Right? Wrong. These conversations are taking place 24 hours per day, and your ability to find them and respond is critical.

So, suppose someone posts something negative on your Wall—what do you do? Easy, right? Just delete it and move on. You want only the positive and fun content around your community. Makes perfect sense. Except if you do this, you'll be committing a cardinal sin of online brand engagement. Even worse, if you have the wrong person managing your Facebook page, and they get into a snit, you'll suffer like Nestle did in March 2010, and your brand might suffer long-term damage. Even now, in late 2011, a Google search for "Nestle" or "Nestle Facebook" shows news reports of Nestle's mismanagement of a Facebook interaction a year and a half old. The person in charge of social media became bitter and sarcastic while publicly posting as the brand.

There are going to be people, both online and offline, who are not happy with your brand, product, or service for one reason or another. Online they can leave comments within your various online outposts, such as your Facebook Page or Group. If the comment isn't violent, overly disruptive, or continual, leave the comment alone. You then have to make the decision whether to respond to the comment. Both decisions have positives and negatives. On one hand, if you do respond, it could spark a never-ending back and forth that might add fuel to a smoldering fire that would have otherwise put itself out. However, on the other side of the coin, if you don't respond, you appear as though you're ignoring the person or complaint the person is bringing to your attention. This could also have an adverse effect. The best advice is to judge each comment on a case-by-case basis. Some you'll respond to, whereas you'll decide that for others it's best to leave them alone. We'll go over some criteria for making those decisions in the next section.

Facebook and Social Media Monitoring

You definitely need to monitor any comments about your executives, company, industry, or competitors. Before you respond, make sure that what you'll write fits with your PR strategies and social media policies. Also, before you decide to respond, consider whether no response might be better. Don't let yourself be baited by people who are trying to provoke you, and never respond if you're emotionally affected by a user's sentiments.

Facebook Pages themselves provide some degree of notification to page admins, and there are other free tools available, such as HyperAlerts (www.hyperalerts.no). Plenty of professional-grade tools, such as Radian6 (www.radian6.com), are available. We suggest you consider setting up a listening and monitoring tool such as Radian6. Just keep in mind that social media monitoring can be complicated and there are dozens of metrics you can keep track of. Make sure the tool you choose can provide the data you need to be insightful about activity in your space.

To Prevent Negativity, Nurture Positivity

One of the great side effects of the Like button (and the lack of a Dislike button) is that most of the connections that happen on Facebook are positive. If you do a good job stimulating likes and comments on your page, you're nurturing positivity. When critics find the Page, if they see overwhelming positivity, they might think twice about attacking. And your biggest fans sometimes defend you publicly, which is the most powerful response.

Summary

Whether you're passionate about being a foodie, a Celtics fan, a fan of Jay-Z, or a customer of a corporation, there is a Page or Group on Facebook for you. You should also try creating a community around something that matters to you. You'd be amazed at how many others will be interested. Niche communities can grow at crazy rates, especially when the members of the community are as passionate as you are.

Combine the information discussed in Chapter 3 and the information provided here to find yourself a few communities to join on Facebook and create your own. Remember the tips provided, and you can move into some of the real benefits of Facebook.

III

Getting the Most Out of Advanced Facebook Features

7

The Power of Local: Facebook Places and Deals

The U.S. Census Bureau in 2007 counted nearly 30 million small businesses, and there are even more worldwide. Many of these are wondering how Facebook can get them more customers and revenue. The good news for local small businesses is that since 2010, Facebook has been creating powerful tools specifically for them to claim their business location and offer discounts to relevant customers. When you consider that the coupon aggregator Groupon brought in $760 million in revenue in 2010 and has an email list of more than 115 million deal-seeking customers, it's clear that this is a big area of opportunity, both for local businesses and Facebook.

The Importance of Locally Oriented Online Marketing

In the history of online marketing, there have been a number of approaches to marketing local businesses and franchises:

- Prior to the Internet, businesses used phone book advertising, local TV advertising, newspapers, and the rest of what's called *traditional marketing*.

- Craigslist began to expand its online classifieds in 2000 in a big way.

- Search marketing advertisers (AdWords, Yahoo!, and similar PPC services) have been able to target their ads to specific locations since they began between 1998 and 2002.

- Google Maps (which was once called Google Local) was added to Google Search in 2005. In 2006, local businesses began showing in search results. Now they are heavily blended with search results, depending on the search phrase.

- Groupon launched in 2008 and is the best known locally oriented deal-of-the-day aggregator, along with Living Social and BuyWithMe.

- Facebook launched Places in 2010 and Deals in 2011.

And local online marketing is big business:

- Google's local advertising opportunity in 2012 is estimated to be $16 billion.

- Local mobile marketing is projected to hit $18 billion in 2016.

- The local online video advertising industry is predicted to reach $1.5 billion by 2012.

- Mobile ad revenues are estimated to top $2.8 billion by 2015.

- Local search revenues are $6 billion in 2011 and projected to hit $8 billion by 2015.

Facebook Check-in Deals is entering a big market to serve these millions of local businesses.

And international expansion is happening quickly. Facebook Deals was launched in Canada and Europe in early 2011, in Australia and South Africa in August 2011, and in Israel in September 2011.

How Does Facebook Check-in Deals Compare to Groupon?

Facebook initially tested a daily deals product in several cities, but decided to end that test in August 2011. Despite its huge network, Facebook didn't feel the model was viable. Likewise, it remains to be seen if Groupon's model is sustainable. Considering that Facebook is moving toward check-in deals created by individual businesses and away from daily deals, we may be talking apples and oranges here. But let's compare these two major players in the local marketing space.

It's been said of the Groupon-type businesses that their power is in their email list—that's how they market small businesses to customers. Groupon has more than 115 million emails and its thousands of salespeople call businesses daily. But Groupon has to continue to advertise and call, as do other companies using that model, which creates significant overhead. Facebook already has 706 million active users and thus possesses an incredible network with which to reach businesses and market them to customers—at no extra cost to Facebook.

Facebook has a few other advantages over Groupon:

- Facebook has a social graph of relationships, many of which are local, which ensures that Check-in Deals will be relevant. Groupon sends offer after offer to email inboxes; most of them are irrelevant to most of the email subscribers and there's no social proof or trust.

- Facebook Credits could, in the future, be tied to Check-in Deals so that Facebook and/or the local businesses doing marketing could get users to take certain actions in exchange for a discount or for free credits.

- Groupon's model requires businesses to offer steep discounts that eliminate profits and may actually cost them money. The promise of customer lifetime value may be an empty one, because the kind of deal seekers who buy only at such deep discounts may be on to the next deal without any loyalty to your business. Facebook can offer more relevant deals of moderate discounts that both allow businesses a margin and weed out the disloyal deal seekers.

Facebook Places

Check-in Deals are built on the back of Places and their other location-tagging features. Facebook users can share their locations as they travel as well as upload content from previous travels (see Figure 7.1).

Figure 7.1 *You can select from a list of places in your current city, choose a different city, or even manually input a place Facebook doesn't know about. You can also see duplicate places, which you have the option to help clean up.*

In August 2011, Facebook added the capability to tag almost anything—photos, status updates, videos—with a location as well. Places can be business locations, and you can claim or create your business/place on Facebook. By creating or controlling a Place on Facebook, you will have more ways to promote and grow your business. When your potential customers can check in at your business, they can tell their friends about it—you enable free word-of-mouth marketing!

There are limitless creative ways to use Facebook Places. For example, Mastercard partnered with Facebook Places in August 2011 and scattered 20 seats from the old Yankee Stadium around New York City. People could scan a QR code on each seat to enter to win Yankees tickets.[1]

Facebook is now also adding a level of location data to virtually everything on the network:

- Users can tag their photos with the location depicted.
- People can tag their statuses if they are posting while traveling.

As Facebook evolves its location features, Places will likely merge into a variety of types of location information users can add to almost any Facebook content.

In your privacy settings, you can control How Tags Work. You can also turn on Profile Review (see Figure 7.2) so that you have to approve any posts you're tagged in before they go on your profile. When you have the new Timeline, you become more conscious of your profile as a representation of your life and values, and you won't want everything your connections might tag you in to be included in that representation.

Figure 7.2   *In your Privacy Settings, you can turn on Profile Review so that you must approve any posts you're tagged in before they show on your profile.*

How Facebook Places Work

Facebook mobile users can check in to a Place, find out which of their friends are nearby and find nearby Places and Deals. As users move about their metro area, if a particular retail store is offering a Check-in Deal, users might see signs about it (provided by the store to alert shoppers). When users check in (via phone or regular computer), an update about it appears on their Wall, in their friends' News Feeds, and on the Place page. Users may choose to tag the friends they're with when they check in. Facebook users can also tag photos, videos, and other content on Facebook with its related location.

Users can share places with their friends by clicking the Share button. The pop-up window lets them share on their Wall, on a friend's Wall, in a Group they're a member of, or in a private message with a small number of friends.

How to Claim Your Business as a Facebook Place

First, search for your business to see whether it's already a Place on Facebook (see Figure 7.3).

Figure 7.3   *Search results for a restaurant in Pawley's Island, SC. This is the first step in claiming your local business on Facebook.*

If you don't find it, it's probably not a Facebook Place yet. Note that Place pages are not the same as Facebook Pages or Community Pages. True Place pages show you a map of the location, a list of friends checked into the place, and a stream of activity from friends who have checked in there in the past. And just to make it more confusing, when you claim your business as a Place, if you already have a Facebook Page for it, you can tie the two together by letting Facebook know that both refer to the same thing.

Figure 7.4 shows the Place named Chive Blossom Cafe, which is restaurant in Pawley's Island, South Carolina. No one has claimed it or connected it to a Page. It also is listed inaccurately in some categories (Home Improvement, for instance).

You can also see that Nearby Places in Figure 7.4 include Caledonia Golf & Fish Club, and if you click that, you'll find it's a Place *and* a Page, as described earlier.

The links in the left column tip us off that this Place has not been claimed by an owner. If it were a local business, it would be good to claim it or notify them if the owner is your friend.

Figure 7.4   *The Place page for the Chive Blossom Cafe. Note from the options in the left column that this Place has not yet been claimed by the restaurant owner.*

If Chive Blossom were our business, we could click Is This Your Business? and it would bring up the window in Figure 7.5.

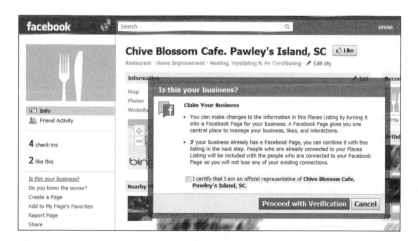

Figure 7.5   *The pop-up that begins the verification process for claiming your business's Place page.*

How to Create a Place

To create a place, you have to first check in while at that location with a Facebook App on a smartphone, or some other web-enabled device, if Facebook Places is available on it. Pull up your Facebook app, tap Places, and then Check In. You will have to share your Current Location. You can also write a description of the location and tag friends. Then click Check In again.

If it's your business, when you go back to Facebook, search for the Place, then claim it as your business.

Figure 7.6 shows that Facebook thinks a Yelp entry is a duplicate of the Pawley's Island Tavern page. In other words, it's asking if that's the same place. To clear up the confusion, click on the checkmark for any places that are the same.

Figure 7.6   *This Page has claimed its place, but Facebook is notifying us in the right column that it thinks it has duplicates in its database—in this case, from Yelp.com.*

Businesses with Multiple Locations

When businesses have multiple locations, Facebook uses a relationship called parent-child to structure everything. Parent pages are the business's main page (see the Walgreens example in Figure 7.7), and child pages (see the Walgreens James Island location in Figure 7.8) are place pages for specific branches or locations. For businesses with hundreds of locations, store managers and franchisees may be required to play a part in monitoring and moderating these child pages.

Figure 7.7   *The Walgreens Page is a parent page, and its Locations tab displays child pages under the map. The Locations page automatically opens to the user's location, or Facebook's best guess of it.*

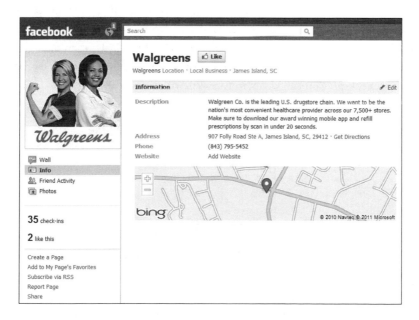

Figure 7.8   *This is a Place page, and specifically, a child page of the Walgreens parent page. This child page is the Walgreens in James Island, SC.*

Note that, at this time, establishing a parent-child relationship between pages can be done only with the help of a Facebook representative. This kind of one-on-one service is only given companies with large Facebook advertising budgets. In the future, though, public features are likely on the way for smaller multilocation businesses.

Facebook Check-in Deals

Facebook Deals are socially enabled digital coupons, and for now, you can create them for free. As a business owner, this gives you the opportunity to motivate customers to check in when they visit, increase awareness of your store through their friends, increase store visits, and grow loyalty. Because of the social aspect built into all of Facebook, your store can become a part of users' conversations with their friends. Many businesses, after initially getting on Facebook, struggle with how to get more attention and fans. Although many businesses use Facebook ads to generate that awareness and fan base, other don't have the budget. Facebook Deals is a strategy that fills that gap.

How Do Facebook Users Find Deals?

You can find deals when you use a smartphone Facebook app. Nearby places that have deals will show a yellow ticket (see Figure 7.9). Some stores may display Facebook Check-in Deal posters. Facebook users also find deals when their friends share them, when businesses advertise them, or by going to https://www.facebook. com/deals/checkin/. You can check in to a store offering a deal.

Figure 7.9   *On the iPhone Facebook app, nearby places that have a yellow ticket are offering Check-in Deals. Tapping on that business reveals more information about the deal.*

What Kinds of Check-in Deals Can You Offer?

There are four types of Check-in Deals:

1. **Individual Deal**—A one-time deal you can offer to new or existing customers.

2. **Friend Deal**—A deal that requires multiple people to check in at once. You can offer this to groups of up to eight people.

3. **Loyalty Deal**—A deal that requires a minimum number (between 2 and 20) of check-ins per customer before they can claim it.

4. **Charity Deal**—A deal wherein your company donates to charity.

How Do You Create a Facebook Deal?

At the bottom of the Deals application is a link you can use, or go straight to http://www.facebook.com/deals/business/. Click Contact Us and enter some information on a contact form (see Figure 7.10) to get started. A Facebook representative will follow up with you to help you create the deal. At this time, there's no self-serve option for creating deals.

Figure 7.10   *The contact form to get started creating a Facebook Deal.*

Some tips to consider when creating your deal:

- You'll need to offer at least 10%–20% to get people to act, or give a gift with the purchase that's worth more than what they bought. You can offer larger discounts, such as 50%, but keep your margin in mind. Facebook Deals has advantages over Groupon that might not make it necessary to give away the farm.

- Keep it simple when designing the deal, and when explaining it. If customers can't understand your offer quickly, they probably won't take advantage of it. This isn't because people are stupid—it's because most people are so busy and distracted. Simple and attractive are the watchwords.

- Get your employees and store ready to redeem the deals. Make sure everyone is informed.

- If you run deals for too long, people will get bored and may not check back on your deals anymore. They'll assume you never update them. And you shouldn't run too many deals at once; when people have too many options, they don't choose any of them. If you have too many similar deals, people may get confused about the differences and give up.

Deal Ideas

Ideas for deals are limited only by your creativity. But here are a few ideas to stimulate you:

- A hotel with a masseuse could set up discounts for unfilled slots. Are sales in the guest shop down lately but you have a big crowd this weekend? How about offering a one-hour-only 20% off sale? Or if you're a hotel that mainly serves business travelers, but you have a new feature or offering, create a deal so customers become aware of it and try it out. Have too much of a certain food in the kitchen? Offer a room service special. Of course, this quick creation and execution of deals requires a framework and empowerment of staff, because they might have to happen at odd times when not all management is available.

- Casinos and resorts have many offerings, so they can target people who are already checked in. Massage, shows, and restaurant specials are things for which many casinos and resorts can offer discounts.

- A bank in Australia offered free movie tickets to anyone who opened a new account. As you can see in this example, the deal offer doesn't even have to be related to what your business offers.

- A 7-11 offered $1.00 Cokes to people who checked in to their Facebook Place.

How Do You Prepare Your Biz for a Deal?

Launching, promoting, and supporting a deal requires planning and preparation. Here are some things to consider:

- Make sure employees know about the deal, and be specific. What is the offer? Is there a limit on the total number of redemptions? Can the same customer use the deal more than once? When does the deal expire? If customers redeem the deal by showing employees their phone screen, how will employees track the claimed deals? If the deal has expired, will you tell all claimants no, or continue to honor it? If you have hundreds of locations, communicate all this to store managers and give them your cell phone number. Be available to answer any questions until they have all the necessary information.

- Clearly communicate all the preceding to customers as well. Do you have a handout or sign with all the details, terms, and conditions?

- Make sure you have enough supply on hand to meet demand. Do you have enough staff ready to handle a bubble in traffic and customer service?

- Make sure your Place page is built out and looks good with your branding, photos, and updates.

- Consider running Facebook ads for the deal. Summarize the deal in your ad and direct it to your Page, Place, or a tab explaining the deal.

Then handle all the customers and cash in on your deal!

Endnotes

1. http://socialnewsdaily.com/1386/mastercard-and-facebook-places-team-up-for-yankees-promotion-in-new-york/

8

Socialize Your Website with Facebook Connect and Social Plug-ins

As we continue to explore Facebook, the majority of the focus is on the ways in which you can use Facebook from within Facebook. Facebook knows that the more useful features it provides, the more you'll come back, the longer you'll stay, and the more people you'll tell about how great it is. Facebook has spent a lot of time building a feature set geared toward addicting you to its service. It's a wonderful loop of engagement. But Facebook is also interested in extending its experience to the rest of the Web, extending that engagement loop to every site on the Internet.

Facebook's social plug-ins, which extend Facebook to the rest of the web, provide more opportunities for you, as a marketer, because they increases your ability to connect with new prospects, current customers, and fans of your brand.

Facebook created Facebook Connect in December 2008. If you've visited practically any major website, or even most top blogs, whether you realize it or not, you've probably seen an implementation of Facebook Connect. More than 2.5 million websites have integrated with Facebook—more than 80 of the top U.S. websites and more than half of the top 100 global websites.

Facebook Connect is a lot more than just a blue "Connect with Facebook" box that lets you sign in with your Facebook credentials instead of registering for the site. Facebook gives a basic and geeky definition of Facebook Connect, calling it "a powerful set of APIs for developers that lets users bring their identity and connections everywhere." Facebook Connect is a powerful tool with a complex set of features that can be integrated into websites. For marketers, integrating Facebook Connect helps to bring more eyes to your website, thus giving you more opportunities to connect and convert, as well as to implement other features within Facebook Connect. Additionally, it provides more resources to the user who visits your website and doesn't need to create a new login just to leave a comment or interact with your website in some other way. Keep in mind that the website using these social plug-ins receives none of the information people provide—it all goes to Facebook, and that people see a personalized experience using Facebook's social graph (the relationship between you and your friends).

In April 2010, Facebook launched Social Plug-ins (http://developers.facebook.com/docs/plugins/), which make implementing Facebook Connect much easier.

Social plug-ins include the following:

- **Like button**—Lets users share your web pages with their friends via their Facebook profile
- **Send button**—Lets users send your content to their friends
- **Comments**—Lets you set up a commenting system on your site for Facebook users
- **Activity Feed**—Shows users what their friends are doing on your site
- **Recommendations**—Gives users personalized recommendations for pages they might like on your site
- **Like box**—Shows your Facebook Page fans and post stream and allows users to like your Facebook Page from your site

- **Registration**—Serves as a simple way for people to sign up for your site

- **Facepile**—Displays pictures of users who have liked your Page or signed up for your site

- **Live Stream**—Lets users interact in real time on your site during a live event

Let's take a look at some of the most popular of these and discuss how you can begin to use the power of Facebook Connect to quickly socialize your website.

First, let us mention how all of these plug-ins will integrate with your site. In every case, you're going to have to copy and paste code into your website. That means you need a basic understanding of HTML and a comfort level with modifying your site. It's just a little bit of code, but you do need to know where to put it. In a few cases, even easier options exist—for example, if your website uses the WordPress platform, you might find a WordPress plug-in custom made for the Facebook social plug-in. If your head is already spinning from this paragraph, you'd better hand these tasks over to your web developer.

Some benefits of using Facebook Connect and its social plug-ins:

- **Easy site login**—Users already logged into Facebook can join your site with one click, authenticating their accounts using Facebook credentials.

- **Socialize**—Make your site social, personalized, and familiar. Demonstrate to new visitors that their trusted friends already like your website. Connected users can view what their friends have viewed, commented on, or reviewed on your site. Social proof builds trust quickly.

- **Look up-to-date**—Social functionality has become so common that without it, your website may feel dull and uninteresting. With the social element added, people have the emotional, familiar experience they've become accustomed to over the past few years.

Adding the Like Button to Your Website

Note that in February 2011, the Like button took over the functionality of what used to be called the Share button. Have you noticed that Facebook likes to change things?

The Like button lets people share your web page with their friends. When someone clicks the Like button on your site, a story appears in the friend's News Feed with a link back to your website. Also, if you provide information about your web page when you create your Like button, this can show up in the Likes and Interests section of the friend's profile, your page could show up in Facebook Search, and advertisers will be able to target people who like your web page.

When you create the Like button with Facebook's handy wizard (see Figure 8.1), you can also add a Send button (see the next section, "Adding the Send Button to Your Website").

Figure 8.1   *The Like button creator also allows you to add a Send button when you create it.*

If you choose to show the number of Likes in your button, note that this number will not be just the number of people that clicked the button; it includes shares, likes, and comments on posts about the URL, and the number of private Inbox messages containing the URL.

When you're ready, click Get Code to get the code you need to insert in your website.

The ability to share stories into your stream is a feature of some more socially forward websites such as Yelp (see Figure 8.2). On Yelp, after you rate a restaurant, you're able to push that review and restaurant information to your Wall as a status update (see Figure 8.3). Whereas the Like Button's can share an article from a website or blog, this story-sharing functionality automatically pushes information to your Facebook Wall while you're interacting on other websites. This is beneficial to the websites that are able to integrate it because the stream story usually carries some of the branding from the website, such as a logo, thus bringing increased brand awareness.

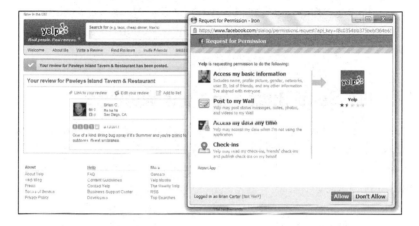

Figure 8.2   *After writing a Yelp review, you have the option to share it on Facebook.*

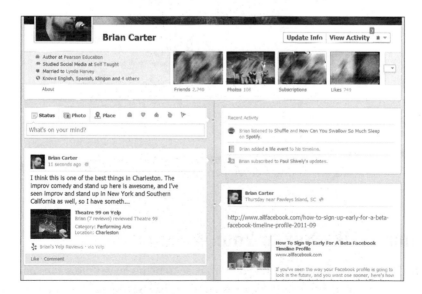

Figure 8.3   *A Yelp review of a Charleston improv theatre, posted on Brian's Facebook Timeline.*

Many websites now use this social functionality to allow you to publish your activity to Facebook. You'll typically see this option with social networks and games that rely on users spreading information to bring awareness of their services.

By linking together the various places where you enjoy hanging out on the Internet, Facebook communicates a lifestream to your friends about what you like. You might worry that if they see too much, people will begin hiding your status updates or unfriending you. Fear not—your friends' News Feeds will see only what they're interested in. What they ignore goes away without them having to take any action.

Adding the Send Button to Your Website

The Send button allows people to send your web page to specific friends, Facebook Groups, and email addresses (see Figure 8.4). They'll have to type in each friend or email address, so the Like button often will reach more of their friends than the Send button does.

Figure 8.4   *The Send button set-up wizard.*

You can find this one at http://developers.facebook.com/docs/reference/plugins/send/.

Adding a Like Box to Your Website

The Like box social plug-in uses your fan base to help you get more fans and customers. Have you ever driven by a restaurant or bar with a big line of people waiting outside? We think, "That must be a good place! We should go, too!" This is *social proof* at work. If you aren't familiar with social proof, it's the idea that when people see how much other people like you or your brand, they're more likely to put aside their skepticism and try you out. They give you a bit more trust initially.

The Like box (see Figure 8.5) gives you a number of options. The simplest implementation is just showing the number of people, along with their faces, who Like your page. But you can also show a stream of recent posts, if you want.

Figure 8.5 *Setting up a Like box, in this case without a post stream.*

This is one of our favorite social plug-ins, but it's not right for everyone. The first question you should ask yourself (and ask as many other people as you can, too) is if the number of fans you have seems impressive. Sure, not every page needs 10,000 or 100,000 fans—in fact, a local niche business might need only a few thousand. But if you think the number looks too small, showing that off might result in social disproof, rather than social proof. "Why don't they have more fans? Maybe they're not that good!"

Adding Facebook Commenting to Your Website

Commenting is one of the most popular Facebook Connect integrations. This feature allows users to choose to sign in with their Facebook account credentials (if you're not already logged in to Facebook, and most people are because you stay logged in unless you deliberately log out) to post comments on a blog or website.

Several blog and commenting platforms (such as Mashable.com, see Figure 8.6) have integrated Facebook Connect into their platforms, which means that users of the blog and commenting system can easily add Facebook Connect to their sites. This has helped to increase engagement with Facebook Connect for commenting. According to one of the most popular blogs in the world, The Huffington Post, it has seen more than one-third of new commenters come through Facebook.

Figure 8.6 *Comments, using the Facebook commenting system, on a Mashable.com post about the Facebook commenting system.*

You can integrate Facebook Comments into your website with the following:

- A WordPress plug-in, if your site is on the WordPress platform

- Disqus, a free blog commenting and discussion system used by sites like CNN, Time, Fox News, and Engadget

- The Facebook Comments social plug-in itself at http://developers. facebook.com/docs/reference/plugins/comments/

Integrating Chat Using the Live Stream

The Live Stream option enables users to chat live side-by-side with either streaming or static content on your website. Users access their Facebook accounts and use the status update feature to carry on conversations.

The Live Stream was first implemented and made uber famous during the presidential inauguration of Barack Obama (see Figure 8.7). During the inauguration, CNN streamed the events live on CNN.com and, using Facebook Connect, allowed you to chat with your friends who were also watching on CNN.com.

Figure 8.7 *CNN used the Live Stream to connect Facebook users with CNN content during the presidential inauguration of Barack Obama. The result: 4,000 status updates per minute and 136 million page views.*

No one could have ever expected how many people would decide to take to CNN.com and start chatting away, sharing this once-in-a-lifetime experience with their friends. According to Mashable.com:

- CNN generated more than 136 million page views.
- More than 600,000 status updates posted through CNN.com to Facebook.
- During the broadcast, more than 4,000 status updates occurred per minute being sent to Facebook from CNN.com.
- During the first minute of President Obama's inaugural speech, 8,500 status updates from CNN.com occurred.

This mind-blowing success led other event planners to turn to Facebook to enable conversations around their event. So far, the Live Feed has been used for the NBA All-Star game, the Michael Jackson Memorial, and a live viewing party of the finale of Bravo's "Real Housewives of New York City," among others.

In the future, we might see many more large events integrate the Facebook Live Stream into their websites. Imagine watching the Olympics, attending a concert, watching the World Series, or watching a movie and chatting LIVE with all your friends who are also enjoying that same experience.

The Live Stream draws out emotion and connects us to something we can relate to. It connects us with our friends during a major event. By enabling this feature, the network hopes that we'll stay on their website longer, and Facebook ensures that we'll interact with their platform more. It also has the spin-off effect, much like Twitter hashtags around events, in that the rest of your network can see your status updates, wonder what you're up to, and hopefully join in on the fun.

Using Facebook for Your Website's Registration and Login System

The concept of single sign-on is something that has continued to float around the Internet as users become increasingly frustrated with the many different websites they have to be signed up for to access content. Such concepts as OpenID have attempted to create a single sign-on that people would use on all the websites they visit. When Facebook created Facebook Connect, it instantly enabled 400+ million users to have a single sign-on (see Figures 8.8 and 8.10).

Figure 8.8   *Now even some major sites such as Yahoo! allow you to log in with Facebook or Google.*

By becoming a single-sign-on resource, Facebook also benefits because users become more reliant on the social network. Because you have the ability to use Facebook to sign into all your favorite websites, you're more likely to interact with Facebook more often.

Another beneficial feature of using Facebook Connect as a single sign-on is that when you log in to Facebook directly or connect with any site that uses Facebook Connect, Facebook signs you in to all the websites that you use Connect with. This means that if you visit five sites that use Facebook Connect, you will not be required to re-enter your login credentials multiple times. Also, when you sign out of any one site, Facebook will sign you out of all websites. This can be helpful if you use a public computer so that you don't have to remember to log in and out of all the websites that you might visit during a browsing session.

As Facebook continues to grow, registration might become one of the most popular features of Facebook Connect.

Setting up the registration is the easy part. There's a wizard for it (see Figure 8.9 and online at http://developers.facebook.com/docs/plugins/registration/), just like the other social plug-ins. Where it gets more complicated is when your programmer takes over—reading the data you get from user sign-ups and integrating that into your website.

Figure 8.9 *A registration form example. You can customize this and add more fields if needed.*

Figure 8.10   *When you click Log In at The Huffington Post, you get a host of login options, including Facebook, Twitter, AOL, and more.*

Creating a Personalized Experience with Facebook Connect

We've only seen glimpses of the capability of Facebook Connect to create a personalized experience. Facebook Connect has the capability to use some of your information, such as age, gender, location, or content that you've uploaded to Facebook, to help create a story just for you. You can go as far as your creativity and your programmers can take you.

To fully understand what creating a personalized experience with Facebook Connect means, it is easiest to learn about how some have chosen to use this feature.

During Shark Week 2009, the Discovery Channel sought to find ways to pull people in to watch its special programming. The Discovery Channel realized that one way to accomplish this would be to reach out into the communities where people are already hanging out. Instead of hoping that they tune in and watch commercials related to Shark Week, the Discovery Channel, with the assistance of C.C. Chapman and his team at Campfire (previously known as the Advance Guard), decided to use Facebook as a digital channel to find potential viewers.

The easy way would be to use a Facebook Ad with a call to action. But what if you could make users feel as though they were in a boat being attacked by a shark?

What if you could make their heart race and make it seem real for them? That would be cool, right? That's exactly what an application called Frenzied Waters created for Shark Week using Facebook Connect. By using information that you've already made available to Facebook, such as biographical information and photos, the Frenzied Waters application created an experience that made you feel as though you were part of the shark attack.

Intel's 2011 Museum of Me (www.intel.com/museumofme/) has been widely applauded as one of the best examples of Facebook Connect personalization yet. After you connect, you are taken through a fictional museum that showcases your photos, your words, your videos, and your friends. Some examples from Brian's Museum of... him... are shown in Figures 8.11 and 8.12. He felt that it was admirably ambitious but that the experience would have been more powerful if he had 500 friends rather than 2,500; and that the approach was a bit too narcissistic. A Museum of Friends exploring your connections with them might be more powerful.

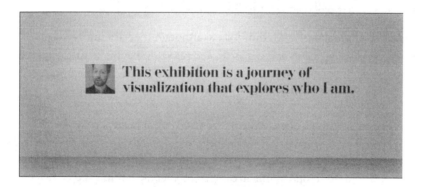

Figure 8.11   *The beginning of Intel's Museum of Me, for Brian.*

Figure 8.12   *The photo section of Intel's Museum of Me.*

What both of these applications accomplish is invoking emotion and bringing you into the experience. This tends to hook you and makes you want to run around and share it with your friends because of how cool it is. This word-of-mouth marketing is the best type of marketing that any brand or product could ask for.

Not Just for the Web

Although much of this chapter's discussion has been about websites, some of the features of Facebook Connect really shine on the iPhone. Facebook Connect has become increasingly popular, especially among applications that offer reviews of entertainment and dining options, such as movies, music, restaurants, bars, and hotels.

Applications such as Flixster, a popular movie-sharing and reviews application, have implemented Facebook Connect so that you can see how your friends on Facebook review a movie. Another popular iPhone application, UrbanSpoon, currently has nearly 6,000 active users per day.

The importance of this is not in the stats, although they are impressive. UrbanSpoon sees Facebook users as *trusted referrals*. People trust referrals by friends more than from any other source. This is the secret sauce for applications such as Flixster and UrbanSpoon (as shown in Figure 8.13) when they implement Facebook Connect.

In a society in which we're inundated with an estimated 35GB of data daily, we need to find ways to weed through all that information. One way is to do exactly what we would do in our offline lives: turn to friends, family, and colleagues for information. Instead of reading what the *New York Times* food critic thinks of the Italian spot across town, you now can turn to UrbanSpoon to see what *your* friends, family, or colleagues thought of it. Was the chicken parmigiana fantastic? Parking easy to find? Service horrible? Your friends on Facebook will tell you instantly. Where the payoff for the application comes in is that because it provides useful and trustworthy information, you'll keep coming back. If you know that you can turn to Flixster to watch movie trailers, find the closest movie theater and showtimes, and learn what your friends thought of the summer's supposed blockbuster, why wouldn't you keep coming back to Flixster?

Figure 8.13 *UrbanSpoon uses Facebook Connect on both its website and its iPhone application. This enables users to read reviews from their friends instead of from users who are unknown to them.*

Summary

As you can see from the examples in this chapter, Facebook Connect and its social plug-ins are powerful tools to integrate into your website, blog, or application. Time and time again it has proven to drive increased traffic and engagement. What's nice about Facebook Connect is that you can select a breadth of options to integrate. You could begin immediately by implementing sharing of content on your website while you work on ways to integrate social filtering into your application and create a personalized experience for your visitors.

One of the most interesting aspects of Facebook Connect is that it provides you with a social graph of your website, application, or service. Because of the information that Facebook knows about every user, you can identify exactly who is interacting with your website. Armed with that information, you can create content, offers, and options geared to that demographic. It is likely that Facebook will continue to expand Facebook Connect to include more options and flexibility.

9

Facebook Credits: Social Currency and Your Business

Virtual currency? Money that works only online? That sounds more like an idea from a Star Trek movie than a practical business strategy, doesn't it? Believe it or not, more than 200 million people have already used Facebook Credits, a currency that exists only on Facebook. Initially it was used to play games such as Farmville and Mafia Wars, but recently, major entertainment and news media companies have been testing it as well. The question is: When should you start considering whether your business can use it? And the answer is: now.

What Are Facebook Credits?

Facebook Credits are a virtual currency used only on Facebook that debuted in May 2009. Ten credits are equal to one dollar. Facebook keeps 30% of all Facebook Credit transactions. Some think that is steep, but Facebook justifies the price by citing Apple's 30% bite of all its App Store subscriptions.

Since July 2011, Facebook Credits are the only approved way to pay for games on Facebook. In fact, developers that don't submit to this might find their apps shut down. Zynga is the biggest game company on Facebook and the biggest success story with Facebook Credits. In 2010, Zynga made a $27.9 million profit on revenue of $597.5 million from Facebook games. Its revenue increased 133% in the first quarter of 2011, and it could exceed $1 billion in revenue in 2011.

As more and more businesses move toward Facebook e-commerce, it's possible Facebook Credits could become one of the payment methods. Christian Taylor, CEO of Payvment, one of the biggest e-commerce store providers, predicted that Facebook Credits would eventually be another way to pay in its system. He said it was a "no brainer."

Could Payvment become the Amazon.com of Facebook? It's certainly possible after it can accept Facebook Credits, and assuming Facebook knocks down the 30% fee. You can see how a virtual goods business might be able to absorb a 30% fee, but that would be the entire profit margin for some e-tailers. Considering that PayPal takes only 3% or less of transactions, you can see that 30% is in a completely different realm. If Facebook wants e-commerce to make a serious move to its platform and to Credits, it will need a much, much lower fee.

How to Get Facebook Credits

Users can obtain Facebook Credits in several ways:

- Pay with a credit card or PayPal within the Facebook Payments tab in your Account Settings or in Facebook games.
- Buy them online or in retail stores such as Kohl's, Target, Best Buy, Radio Shack, and Game Stop (Topps, the well-known trading card company, bought the Facebook gift card provider GMG in July 2011).
- Exchange other gift cards for Facebook Credits with Plastic Jungle at http://apps.facebook.com/plasticjungle/?ref=credits_landing.

- Earn free Credits by checking in at participating stores through the ShopKick iPhone app or by checking into other locations through the game Booyah!

- Pay on your mobile phone—you'll be billed through your mobile carrier.

Uses of Facebook Credits Beyond Games

Certainly, Facebook Credits are best known for their use in social games played by people tending to fake farms, pets, and westward journeys. But in 2011 a number of big entertainment and news companies began testing Facebook Credits as well. Let's start by taking a look at some innovative firms that are already earning revenue with Facebook Credits.

Movies and Television

Miramax launched a Facebook app called Miramax eXperience (see Figure 9.1) that allows you to watch free clips and rent movies instantly. You can stream any of 20 films for 48 hours for just 30 Facebook Credits ($3.00 USD). What's even more interesting is that Miramax sees this as the first iteration of a bigger project that will enable people to watch any movie from the cloud across all their devices. Miramax also has an iPad app at http://apps.miramax.com/ipad.html.

The Big Lebowski can be rented from its Facebook page (see Figure 9.2). What's more, viewers can like and comment on memorable quotes from the movie, as well as see what other fans and friends have said while watching.

Here's a smart idea: Transforming the often-isolating experience of watching a movie into a social event. In a dark theater, texting, Tweeting, and Facebooking can annoy others. But with this app, viewers can watch at home and comment alongside their peers. *The Big Lebowski*, a cult classic, is a perfect movie for this venture. It makes sense to offer other much-loved films to their hardcore fans, such as *Monty Python and the Holy Grail* or *The Princess Bride*. Viewers who invite up to five friends to rent the film can get each of them a $1 discount. Normally, the films rent for $3 or 30 Facebook Credits for 48 hours.

Figure 9.1   *The Miramax eXperience, a way to watch movies online and pay only with Facebook Credits.*

Figure 9.2   *Fans of The Big Lebowski can like and comment on scenes and quotes, and earn credits for their friends by inviting them to watch, too.*

Our friends across the pond are getting involved, too, offering a number of TV shows for purchase via Facebook apps:

- Viewers of the U.K.'s *Big Brother* TV reality show can vote on Facebook to expel irritating housemates if they pay for that vote with Facebook Credits.

- The British Broadcasting Corporation was the first to offer a TV show for purchase on Facebook—*Doctor Who* (see Figure 9.3; the longest running and most successful science fiction television show in history), in July 2011.

- BBC Worldwide is offering episodes of its popular *Top Gear* show on Facebook for 15 credits each, $1.50 USD.

Figure 9.3   *Facebook users can stream Doctor Who episodes in exchange for Facebook Credits.*

News Media and Facebook Credits

Print news media, severely affected by the Internet, have been casting about for new business models for years. The industry has lost a number of newspapers and a fifth of its workforce to bankruptcies and cutbacks. As far back as 2002, publications such as *The Financial Times* and *The New York Times* have used paywalls to require payment in exchange for online reading. The *Wall Street Journal* generates $65 million per year from its online readership.

Similarly, new media are now experimenting with Like Gates, which require a like before you can read, and Facebook Credit paywalls. Because they need more fans, the *New Yorker* used a Like Gate, dangling an essay by a Pulitzer Prize finalist in exchange for likes. Other media, like *Forbes*, are considering a payment wall using Facebook Credits for access to their Facebook editions.

The Music Industry and Facebook Credits

Like the dilemma faced by print media, the music industry's troubled business model has been well publicized. But innovative artists such as Radiohead are finding creative solutions: When the band released its album *In Rainbows*, it allowed fans to set their own download prices. Although they could download it for free,[1] the average fan paid about four British pounds.[2] Moreover, the press coverage of the band's novel approach helped propel *In Rainbows* to become the best-selling vinyl album of 2008. Even though the band did not distribute the album through a record label, Radiohead's profits were similar to what it had made previously using a traditional business model.1.   http://en.wikipedia.org/wiki/In_Rainbows#Distribution2. http://entertainment.timesonline.co.uk/tol/arts_and_entertainment/music/article2633798.ece

What's the point? Think outside the box—especially when your box (your industry's business model) is falling apart. Leveraging Facebook and Credits is a smart new model to test.

Widespread Panic and David Gray are two musical acts already experimenting with Facebook apps and credits.

Widespread Panic is a jam band much loved by Grateful Dead fans. The band played a live show that was broadcast by *Austin City Limits* and socially broadcast on Facebook by Milyoni, a social e-commerce application company. Fans paid 50 Facebook Credits ($5 USD) to view it on Facebook.

Did it work? Here are the results:

- 2,300 people from 19 countries attended.
- 1,900 comments were posted during the show.
- 50% of viewers joined via word of mouth after it was already in progress.

- 100% paid with Facebook Credits, mostly purchased via PayPal.

- Widespread Panic gained 20,000 Facebook fans, about a 10% gain compared to its previous fan base.

Analytics for Facebook Credits

Elsewhere in this book we discuss analytics for both Facebook Pages and your website. Facebook supplies even more analytics, specifically for Facebook Credits (see Figure 9.4).

Figure 9.4   *Analytics for Facebook Credits.*

Right now you can use it to see spending, chargebacks, and refunds over time.

Takeaways

As you can see, it's still early in the life of Facebook Credits, but they're no longer just for games. Chances are, use of Credits will move into more mainstream business.

So for your business, the first question is: Can you and should you sell things on Facebook? If you don't have physical goods, do you have valuable electronic content (videos, ebooks, whitepapers, reports, and the like) you might want to sell on Facebook? If so, the capability to merge this selling activity with social liking and sharing could represent a powerful and profitable marketing strategy for your business.

Endnotes

1. http://en.wikipedia.org/wiki/In_Rainbows#Distribution
2. http://entertainment.timesonline.co.uk/tol/arts_and_entertainment/music/article2633798.ece

IV

Role Models and Predictions

10

Best in Class Facebook Pages

What makes a great Facebook Page? Getting lots of exposure in fans' News Feeds and a high degree of fan interaction require listening and creative stimulation—are you getting enough response? Pages offer many customization options—are you using these features in the best possible ways? If you're a business that can track a return on your social media investment, are you profiting from your Facebook marketing campaigns? This chapter offers examples of businesses that are doing a great job in each of these areas.

In this third edition of *Facebook Marketing*, we've divided our Best in Class pages into several categories of achievement. It's almost like the Oscars, but nerdier.

- Best Fan Interaction
- Best Use of Facebook Features
- Best Revenue and ROI

This approach allows us to highlight winners of all sizes, from local small businesses to Fortune 500 corporations. Regardless of category, each of the Pages discussed is given a fan interaction score. As you'll see, not every page does well in every category—for example, some of those with exciting Welcome tabs are not doing a great job with engagement.

Best Fan Interaction

Engagement is a huge deal, because without it, your fans won't see your Page's posts in their News Feeds anymore. We reviewed 20 Facebook Pages of all sizes and summarized them in Table 10.1.

Table 10.1 Twenty-One Facebook Pages and Their Level of Engagement

Page	Fans	Max Interactions	Estimated Visibility	Score
Rosehall Kennel	1,484	66	6,600	445%
I Wish I Were Diving	14,408	550	55,000	382%
Zion National Park	2,512	95	9,500	378%
WUSLU	9,218	106	10,600	115%
Cowboys & Aliens	279,991	2,600	260,000	93%
Baseball Roses	5,485	49	4,900	89%
Brian Solis	13,946	123	12,300	88%
Ellen	5,642,105	46,000	4,600,000	82%
Gavin Newsom	100,696	640	64,000	64%
Vin Diesel	27,482,176	169,000	16,900,000	61%
VW Bus	28,254	145	14,500	51%
The White House	1,136,460	5,800	580,000	51%

Page	Fans	Max Interactions	Estimated Visibility	Score
Gary Vaynerchuck	68,346	240	24,000	35%
Lady Gaga	42,893,204	131,000	13,100,000	31%
HubSpot	31,501	84	8,400	27%
Barack Obama	22,746,832	49,000	4,900,000	22%
Coca-Cola	33,906,263	52,000	5,200,000	15%
KLOVE	834,515	1,200	120,000	14%
VW	832,895	1,000	100,000	12%
Spartan Race	518,588	410	41,000	8%
Mashable	582,962	337	33,700	6%
Zappos Men	7,710	2	200	3%

- **Fans** is their total fan count.
- **Maximum Interactions** is the sum of likes and comments on the Page's most engaging recent post.
- **Estimated Visibility** is an estimate of how many fans they would reach if their most engaging post had a 1% feedback rate.
- **Score** is a grade of how well they are doing with fan responses compared to their fan count. Note that, although in the scores throughout the chapter I showed a maximum possible score of 100%, in the table I allowed scores to go above 100%. This measure shows you just *how* outstanding some of the Pages are in the engagement category.

I Wish I Were Diving

I Wish I Were Diving is a scuba diving travel and deal-focused Facebook Page. Their Welcome tab is nothing to write home about, but they do have one, and it does the basics: it tells you to like the Page and why. We do think they need a better video, because the guy narrating sounds like he needs Prozac, but we do give them props for going further than most companies do in setting up their Facebook Pages.

What this Page does best is engagement (see Figure 10.1). You can see they got a 100% in their engagement score. The simple scale we use only goes up to 100%, but they were the second most engaging of all the Pages we reviewed.

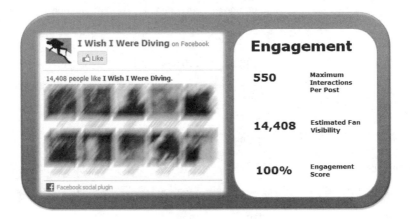

Figure 10.1 *Fan count and engagement stats for the I Wish I Were Diving Page.*

How do they get such great engagement? They ask questions and ask for likes. Here is a typical post: "Do you like this diving photo? Please click Like. Have you had a similar up-close experience with a beautiful school of fish? Tell us about it via a comment and have a great day!" It's not rocket science, nor is it Ernest Hemingway, but if you tell people what you want (in this case, likes and comments), you're a lot more likely to get it.

Vin Diesel

Vin Diesel is an international movie star best known for his *Fast & Furious* franchise movies. Many of his movies do well with a cross-section of society. So, it isn't much surprise to see that Vin Diesel is active on Facebook with more than 27 million fans as of September 2011.

The reason why Vin was chosen as one of the "Best in Class" is not because the Page is that innovative compared to many of the other Pages that are featured in this book or that can be found on Facebook. The primary reason Vin Diesel was chosen is because of how active he is in simply being human. Vin uses the basic features of the platform, such as the Photos, Videos, Discussions, and the Wall, to communicate directly with his fans and provide them with a behind-the-scenes glimpse of his life (see Figure 10.2).

Figure 10.2 *Vin Diesel's Facebook Page.*

Vin actively posts approximately once per day or every couple days on his Wall. He has uploaded a bunch of photos that are behind-the-scenes shots of Vin filming various movies, at various events, and just hanging out. Vin has also uploaded several videos in which he answers commonly asked questions from fans and talks about his travels or anything else on his mind. Vin also keeps his Events tab updated with all of his appearances, such as interviews, public appearances, movies hitting theaters, and more.

What makes this Page so different from many of the others is that it is actually Vin Diesel. It would be easy for Vin to have an assistant manage his presence on Facebook, but instead he does it himself. By doing this, he connects directly with his fans. It allows fans to connect with Vin when, if not for Facebook or other social networks, fans would probably never have the opportunity to connect with their favorite celebrity. Granted, Vin is only a single person, so he doesn't have the ability to answer every question or comment that is sent to him. But, by being consistently active, he shows his fans that he really does care about connecting with them, and that's a big reason for his great engagement score (see Figure 10.3).

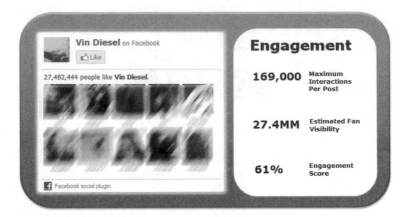

Figure 10.3   *Fan count and engagement stats for Vin Diesel's Facebook Page.*

The Ellen DeGeneres Show

The *Ellen DeGeneres Show* is a television talk show that draws millions of daily viewers. Ellen has developed a strong fan base because she appeals to a lot of people and brings diverse guests to the show. It is no surprise that her Facebook Page, as of September 2011, has more than 5.6 million fans.

Although the *Ellen* staff isn't active on its Wall like some of our other "Best in Class" pages, they are very active in keeping the Page updated with new content. Every Friday they post fan photos, and these photo posts get far and away the biggest response from her fans. Videos get the second most response. In fact, although she scores well based on her photo posts (see Figure 10.4), if we had looked only at her status updates for interaction, she would have only a 5% engagement score. But this is fine—it's a good idea to use multiple post types. Just be aware of which types get you the most response and visibility in case you want to reach more people with a particular post.

One of the first things you notice when landing on the Page is your chance to win tickets to be on her show (see Figure 10.5). When you click any of the titles, it brings you to a vibrant landing page on the *Ellen DeGeneres Show* website that provides you with a description and has a short form for you to fill out. In case you land on that page without coming from the Facebook Page, each landing page actively promotes the show's presence on both Twitter and Facebook.

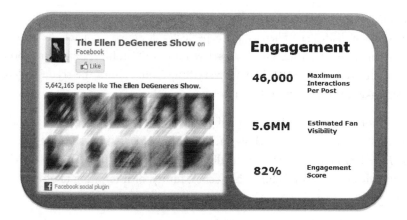

Figure 10.4   *Fan count and engagement stats for Ellen's Facebook Page.*

Figure 10.5   *On her Welcome tab, fans can enter to win tickets to the taping of Ellen's show.*

The *Ellen* team has also created an EllenTV tab that is an extension of the show's blog on its website. The EllenTV tab is perfectly designed to match the look and feel of the show's website. This is an active blog with multiple daily posts. Some days there are 5–10 posts providing everything from behind-the-scenes videos to sweepstakes information to show information.

In addition to all this content being shared on the Facebook Page, you can also find a handful of videos from the show and tons of photos that have been uploaded. The *Ellen* team creates a new photo album every month titled "What You Missed in [Month][Year]" with behind-the-scenes, funny, or interesting photos from the filming of the show.

The *Ellen* show also has an active Discussion area in which fans regularly talk with one another, offer advice, ask questions, and keep a vibrant community going. This is pretty exceptional, because most Pages are unable to get activity in the Discussions tab, and it seems to have gotten more difficult as Facebook has emphasized the News Feed more and more.

Best Use of Facebook Features

Spartan Race

The Spartan Race is crazy, we'll admit, but it is very popular! Founded in 2005, they put on a series of competitive obstacle course events of increasing difficulty, from the 3-mile Spartan Sprint to the 48-hour Spartan Death Race.

They aren't doing a great job with engagement (see Figure 10.6). But their Welcome tab, created with the assistance of the Lujure Assemblyline product (www.lujure.com), kicks butt. As soon as you get there, a killer hard-hitting video starts to play automatically and begins to intimidate and challenge you into participating (see Figure 10.7). This is a great example of how to make your website and Facebook presentation consistent.

The Welcome tab is also their Sign Up tab. You can register for a race or sign up for their email, which delivers daily Spartan workouts. They've also loaded every race into their Events tab. This is a great demonstration of the use of every Facebook Page feature. Now, let's see if they can figure out engagement!

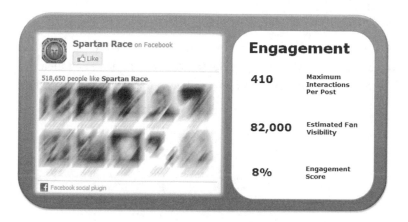

Figure 10.6   *Fan count and engagement stats for the Spartan Race Facebook Page.*

Figure 10.7   *The Spartan Race Welcome tab looks great and starts intimidating and inspiring you as soon as you land on it.*

Volkswagen

Volkswagen (VW) left the pack behind when it launched its Pages. VW created individual Pages for each of its vehicles (a total of 14 to date) and then rolled those up to a corporate VW page. You can see a few of the many vehicle Pages they've created in Figure 10.8.

Figure 10.8 *Just a few of the Pages VW manages for each of its cars.*

VW previously had an innovative Facebook application (see Figure 10.9) that analyzed "you" by analyzing your profile information. Based on that information, it recommended a VW vehicle that it believes will be best suited for you. How cool is that? Although VW doesn't feature it anymore, you can still use the app by going to http://apps.facebook.com/meetthevolkswagens.

Now VW has moved to a strategy of new promotions. For example, the landing tab for the VW page now announces the new 2012 Beetle.

Elsewhere on the VW corporate Page you can find tons of photos and videos that have been uploaded and an active Events tab that shows all upcoming VW events.

VW also encourages fans to upload their own photos and videos as a way of extending the community. As of March 2010, this community had grown to more than 832,000 fans. These fans are passionate and engaged on the Wall of the VW page.

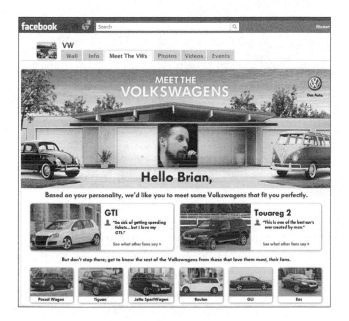

Figure 10.9 *The Meet the Volkswagens application.*

Each individual vehicle line Page has, depending on the popularity of the vehicle, upward of tens of thousands of fans that actively upload photos, videos, and post to the Page's Wall. Each vehicle line Page also contains a customized advertisement for the vehicle that if clicked brings you over to the VW website and onto that specific vehicle Page, where you can see more information and pricing, and contact a dealer.

Although VW's engagement score (see Figure 10.10) was only 12% (max of about 1,000 comments despite 832,000 fans), it does better on some of its specific vehicle Pages. For example, VW scores 51% on its VW Bus Facebook Page (up to 149 comments from 28,254 fans).

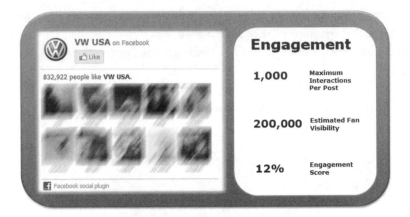

Figure 10.10   *Fan count and engagement stats for the VW USA Facebook Page.*

Barack Obama

During his presidential campaign, Barack Obama and campaign manager, David Plouffe, turned to social media as a way to reach out to constituents. It allowed Obama to hear the American public's concerns on platforms that they felt comfortable sharing on. Obama's use of social media and his activation of people to help spread the campaign's message is one of the primary ways he was so wildly successful in raising funds and defeating Senator John McCain by a large margin on election day.

One of the primary tools that Obama and his team used was a Facebook Page (www.facebook.com/barackobama), as shown in Figure 10.11. After Obama became the 44th president of the United States, his team continued to use Facebook as a means of communicating directly with the American public. The Facebook Page is *very* active, and there is usually one update or so per day. What is different from many of the other pages that were chosen as part of the "Best in Class" group is that the Obama Page is closed to allowing fans to publish or share on the Wall. This is expected and doesn't come as any surprise to most people. Everyone can still comment on, like, or share any update that the Obama administration publishes, though.

Unfortunately, the Obama Page doesn't rate as one of the most engaging for fans. This is a common occurrence when you see a Page that still pushes content without asking for interaction. Only one recent post asks a question, and not coincidentally, it's one of the most liked and commented ones. Too many of the posts are simply quotes or photos. These are fine to post, but it's always a good idea to add a call to action to such posts: "What do you think about this quote?" or "Click Like if you agree!"

Figure 10.11   *United States President Barack Obama's Facebook Page.*

But Obama's page does a great job with some very important political functions:

- **The Are You In? tab** is a way of getting a commitment to support Obama in 2012. Social scientists have found that people tend to stay consistent with their commitments.

- **The Donate tab** (see Figure 10.12) helps them raise money.

- **The Store tab** allows them to sell promotional t-shirts, stickers, and more for both social proof (when we see people using or liking something, we're more likely to use or like it ourselves) and fund-raising purposes.

One of the more interesting uses was when President Obama held an online town hall and the White House took questions on a section of the White House site; then the president selected certain questions to answer during this town hall. Although the online town hall did not take place exclusively on Facebook, the video was posted to Facebook (see Figure 10.13). Overall, the online town hall had 92,937 people who submitted 103,978 questions and cast 1,782,650 votes, according to the White House.

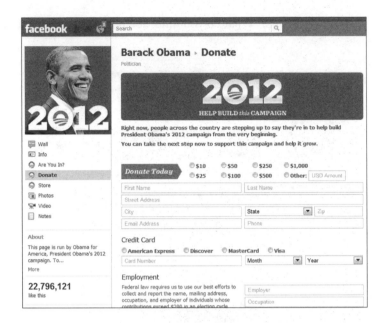

Figure 10.12 *President Barack Obama's Page uses a custom tab to raise funds for his 2012 campaign.*

Figure 10.13 *An example of a video posted to the Facebook Page by President Barack Obama's team. This video was of an online town hall that the president conducted.*

Although the Page is not necessarily different or innovative—if anything, it is more restrictive than other pages—it is interesting to see President Obama and the White House staff continuing to utilize this as a main source of communicating directly with the American people. However, it would help his engagement score (see Figure 10.14) to ask more questions, which would double as great research for his re-election team.

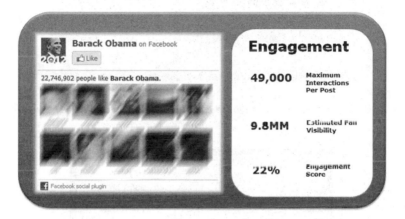

Figure 10.14   *Fan count and engagement stats for Barack Obama's Facebook Page.*

Best Revenue and ROI

Rosehall Kennel

Rosehall Kennel breeds and sells German Shepherd puppies. This very small business actually has the best engagement *and* profitability of all the pages we surveyed.

With a very small and targeted ad spend, owner Eliot Roberts (a student in Brian's FanReach course who reported this via private email) achieved a 3,991% ROI. In eight months, the kennel brought in $13,500 from just a $330 ad spend. It helps that the average sale is $1,350—high-priced products can produce very high profits, especially when the ad cost in the niche is low. He has had less pressure to discount, it takes the kennel less time to completely sell a litter, and buyers are more educated and have more reasonable expectations.

Eliot also reports an average post feedback rate of 1.55%, which is an exceptional engagement rate (see Figure 10.15). Check out Figure 10.16—Eliot has taken an already cute puppy photo and added an innocuous thought bubble that makes it even cuter. How can you get more creative with the photos you're posting?

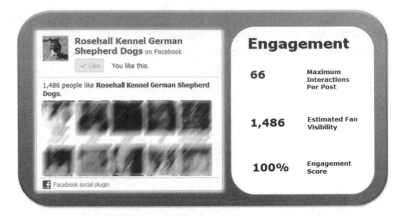

Figure 10.15 *Fan count and engagement stats for Rosehall Kennel's Facebook Page.*

Figure 10.16 *This picture got 28 interactions from just 1,488 fans. The feedback rate here was likely close to 2.0%.*

Baseball Roses

Mark Ellingson started an unusual company in 2010, a hybrid of sorts. He sells artificial roses made of real baseballs and softballs (see Figure 10.17). His Facebook ad campaigns grew his fan base and he achieved a 300% ROI on sales from those fans. This company and Rosehall Kennel's experience will be heartening to the millions of small businesses out there and even more entrepreneurs who need affordable ways to launch their dream businesses.

Figure 10.17   *The Baseball Roses Welcome tab.*

An interesting corollary: Google AdWords advertising did not produce a positive ROI for him, but Facebook did. This makes sense because search marketing is great at fulfilling demand, but no one knows about baseball roses, so no one is searching for them. However, Mark was able to find fans who "liked" baseball, and many of them loved his product idea. That means if your product or service is new or different, Facebook might work better for you than search marketing.

Baseball Roses also does a good job with tabs. It has a solid landing tab (see Figure 10.17), an email signup, and a nice Live Online Help feature powered by SnapEngage.

Overall, Baseball Roses is a winner: profits from its Facebook ad spend, a very high level of engagement (see Figure 10.18), and good use of Facebook features and tabs.

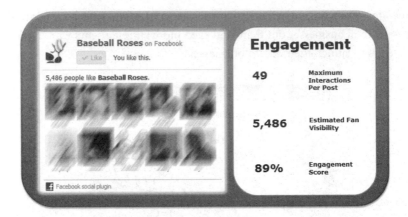

Figure 10.18 *Fan count and engagement stats for the Baseball Roses Facebook Page.*

Lessons Learned from the "Best in Class"

Some of those that made the "Best in Class" are celebrities, politicians, or well-known brands. As with their other web presences, you'd expect these groups of people or companies to have well-designed and managed portals. But you can see that not all of them have figured out Facebook engagement, and some might not be measuring their Facebook profitability.

Most of the tools that even the bigger brands used are available to you. Many of them are built into the Facebook platform. Tab-building tools from companies such as Lujure or Involver can help you look great without expert help or lots of cash.

This is what is different with how these people and companies use Facebook versus their many other web presences. Many of us couldn't afford or don't have enough content to have the scale of website that President Obama or VW do. It would either be too costly to build or we simply don't need that many features on our websites. Many websites contain static information that rarely changes.

Facebook is different because it is constantly evolving. Facebook is real time. The basic features built into the platform allow all of us to integrate various forms of communications tools to reach out and build communities. It is exactly what all those who were featured as among the "Best in Class" have done in various ways. Some have teams manage their content for them, such as President Obama, whereas others get into the trenches themselves and stay directly connected, such as Vin Diesel.

All of them use the same tools that all of us can use. They're not receiving special access to features that aren't available to everyone else. The only difference is that their growth rates are much different than the majority of Facebook Pages. Don't get caught up in the numbers, though. Although impressive, they represent only a small portion of their overall fan bases. Also, the size of the number isn't what matters. What matters is having the number of right followers or fans for your brand, and whether you can keep those fans engaged. Therefore, you should analyze these Pages to see how you can improve your presence or the presence of your brand or your clients' brands. Take segments of what you like from each of these and other Pages to create a dynamic presence on Facebook.

To help you get started with this analysis, here are four takeaways:

1. **Use all available features.** Facebook provides a number of tools that help you to build a solid 360-degree view of yourself or your brand. Use them to their fullest. Upload photos, videos, and events. Make use of custom tabs and landing tabs to impress new visitors and achieve your other objectives.

2. **Promote your page.** Include your Page in your email signature, in your email marketing, on your other social media presences, on your marketing materials such as brochures, and other appropriate places. Come up with creative ways to expose your presence. As we saw with Rosehall Kennel and Baseball Roses, smart ad targeting can yield profitability even for small businesses.

3. **Interact.** If people are taking time out of their schedules to stop by your Page and leave a comment or upload a picture, you can take the time to comment back. Keep your feedback rates up with questions and calls to action in posts. Never post any content without asking them to respond in some way.

4. **Be helpful.** As you build your community, provide members with a variety of types of content and interact often with them; you'll want to be as helpful as possible. Being repeatedly helpful to your community can bring members back often. Don't always just promote your stuff; promote others. Share interesting links that are pertinent to your community. Subscribe to some of your fans' blogs, and occasionally promote their relevant posts to the community. Not only will those fans be appreciative, but they'll also be more likely to help promote your Page because it is useful to them.

By combining these tips with your own takeaways, you can start to develop a solid strategy for your Page so that you can help to grow it to be as successful as those featured here.

Finally, hundreds of great Pages exist that aren't mentioned here. If you come across other great Pages that you think we could all learn from, contact us and share it. As this book reaches bookshelves, many new Pages will take these concepts and blow them out of the water. Let us know about them!

11

What's Next for Facebook

What's next for Facebook drives much speculation across the blogosphere and social media landscape. At times, there can be so much buzz that it drives mainstream media attention as well. Facebook is one of the most popular websites in the world, so its community analyzes its every move with a microscope. When new team members, especially at the project lead level, join or leave Facebook, their previous experience is critiqued and analyzed as to what that might mean for the future of Facebook. Speculation runs the gamut from the basics of what new features the development team might, or should, be working on to when it will go public. Beyond speculation, as soon as a new update is released, a team member conducts an interview, or an announcement is made, it spreads through the blogosphere like wildfire. If it's a new feature implementation, almost immediately you'll find a dozen plus Facebook Pages pop up crying foul on the new features. In fact, Facebook expects a bit of complaint about each change, so it ignores feedback for 48 hours and then listens!

This level of scrutiny is expected as Facebook grows at a blistering pace, adding hundreds of thousands of new users every day. Also, as social media continues to mature, the entire industry is put under a microscope. Every little move from a social network, large or small, causes a ripple effect of conversations, blog posts, media stories, cheers, and jeers. Rather quickly, the community calms down, acclimates to the new feature set, and waits for the next story to drop. Because Facebook is the largest social network, it is no surprise that it comes under the most scrutiny.

Besides the scrutiny it comes under by the community, you, as a marketer, should immediately start exploring all new features when they're released to discover how they may be helpful to your activity on Facebook. Of course, not every feature will be useful to you from a marketing perspective. But you should carefully analyze all new features to see how they might be leveraged to improve your ability to develop, connect, and engage with your community.

In this book, we have laid out a detailed overview of Facebook, along with actionable information that can be used personally, professionally, and within your company. By the time you read this book, we would expect several of the features to have changed. That's what makes this chapter the most fun. In the closing pages of this book, we want to try shaking the crystal ball to predict what's next for Facebook. We bet you didn't realize you could shake crystal balls. Yes, much like Magic 8-Balls, as long as you don't drop them, they can tell you exactly what's next for social networks.

It is a question that's asked often and one that we want to address. Just as some of the features throughout this book will have changed by the time you read this chapter, we expect that some of these questions will have also been answered. As Justin was writing the second edition of this book, one of his predictions for this chapter was that Facebook would acquire FriendFeed. In 2009, Facebook announced the purchase of FriendFeed for approximately $47.5 million. Alas, it is almost impossible to keep up with this speeding bullet that we call a social network. We've constantly revisited this book to update stats, features, or other changes made to the network.

Going Public

A recurring question as Facebook continues to grow is whether it will go public. On the surface, all things point to the fact that sometime in the near future Facebook will either go public or be purchased. We tend to think that Facebook will lean toward going public. First, it is a powerful and large enough company that only a few companies out there could afford to purchase it. Second, there are no reasons for Facebook to want to sell. It's growing at a fast rate on its own, has no problems raising money, and is in the position in which it can actually make purchases of other companies instead of the other way around. Third, Facebook and Mark Zuckerberg have their own way of doing things and have a fair amount of pride about that and their success.

Facebook has already gone through several rounds of funding; in its latest round in January 2011, it raised $450 million from Goldman Sachs and $50 million from Digital Sky Technologies. As part of the deal, Goldman Sachs will help Facebook raise $1.5 billion more. Facebook was valued at $100 billion in June 2011, up from a $50 billion valuation in January 2011. Altogether, Facebook has raised $800 million over five rounds of funding. It purchased FriendFeed in August 2009 for $47.5 million, and purchased Parakey in July 2007. In February 2009, Facebook invested a seed round of $350,000 in LuckyCal, a service that, based on multiple sources of information, predicts where you're going to be and finds useful and entertaining things for you to do while you're there.

Facebook has gone on an acquisition spree, including companies that import contacts, manage photos, own patents; enable forums, private conversations, mobile check-ins, group messaging, and mobile advertising; make travel recommendations, host and share files, develop mobile apps, and design software. Whether for talent acquisition, to block competition, or to increase functionality, there's no question Facebook is thinking big.

It's not as if Facebook is only raising funds and making investments and purchases. According to the *Wall Street Journal*, Facebook was expected to bring in revenues of approximately $710 million during 2010, but ultimately brought in $1.86 billion. Facebook's 2011 revenues are expected to be as high as $4 billion.

As if funding, investment, and purchasing information isn't enough, in April 2009 when then-Chief Financial Officer Gideon Yu left Facebook, it started a new search for an executive with "public company experience" at the top of its list of requirements. In June 2009, Facebook announced that David Ebersman would take the helm as the third CFO in three years at Facebook. Previous to Facebook, Ebersman served as CFO at Genentech, a biotech giant, for the four years leading up to its $46.8 billion sale to Roche Holding, according to a *BusinessWeek* article.

All signs point toward Facebook going public in the near future. When Facebook does an IPO, it is possible, depending on the market conditions at the time, that we could see its stock price rival that of the near untouchable Google.

How does this affect you as a marketer? Well, as someone who just finished reading several hundred pages about how you should jump into Facebook with both feet and start allocating your precious time to the social network, any corporate movements—especially moving toward acquisition or IPO—should be of interest to you. Additionally, as Facebook grows larger, either through organic growth, acquisition, or an IPO, potentially tens of millions more people will join the social network. Many of them may be your future or current customers.

Acquisitions

In the second edition of this book, Justin wondered whether Twitter or LinkedIn might be on Facebook's acquisition list. Neither of those predictions came true, and LinkedIn went public in January 2011.

Justin also wondered whether Facebook might decide to begin acquiring smaller companies that provide niche feature sets that the network wants to integrate. This is similar to the strategy we have seen from Google over the years. Google has become known for starting to build a new feature and then seeking out a company to acquire that does it better. Google then focuses on integrating those features. Using this strategy, Google has made dozens of investments and even more acquisitions. This prediction was dead on, as Facebook, over the next two years, acquired 13 small companies and the patents of yet another company.

We expect that trend to continue as Facebook adds innovative features and stops new competitors from impinging on Facebook's ownership of any of its current functionality.

What about mergers? One would hope that the failure of the AOL–Time Warner merger would lead to caution. But AOL was a property on the decline with an obsolete business model, whereas Facebook is a thriving social network in its prime. We wonder whether a company such as Facebook or Google will ever merge with a major news organization—and if it would be a good idea.

Integrating More Professionalism and Control

One of the fastest growing demographics within Facebook is the 35 to 55+ age group. When Facebook first opened its doors, the features were built around appealing to students. Features such as photo sharing, video sharing, status updates, commenting, and email have become the foundation of Facebook. But as the network continues to grow, it is attracting more adults who want more professional tools and features integrated and more control over how and with whom they share. Facebook has answered the call with more sophisticated privacy controls for friend lists and everything you share on Facebook. It also now is very easy to see exactly who sees each of your posts (see Figure 11.1).

Figure 11.1   *Clicking the people drop-down next to any of your posts shows exactly who is able to see it.*

Additionally, Facebook should integrate more professional options, such as those offered in LinkedIn. LinkedIn continues to be the most popular professional social network with more than 60 million users and growing. LinkedIn enables users to provide recommendations, build an exportable resume, download Vcards, and post job announcements. It offers several other features that appeal solely to the professional. Although Facebook would continue to grow without integrating similar features, it would reach deeper into its user base if it did. It would keep Facebook users on the network longer and, in turn, users would share more data with Facebook. Furthermore, it would allow Facebook to continue separating itself from the rest of the pack of other social networks.

The News Feed and EdgeRank

EdgeRank has become so important that third-party businesses are being built on measuring your effectiveness with it (EdgeRankChecker.com) and determining how to improve your results with it (PageLever.com). Facebook continues to experiment with how to best filter content to users from their friends and favorite Pages. Recently, Facebook was testing a headlines feature that also seemed to use EdgeRank. The question going forward is: Will Facebook improve EdgeRank, or jettison it in favor of something else?

Further, will Facebook begin to incorporate ways to see what is most popular across all of Facebook? At this time, everything you see on Facebook is personalized, but tens of thousands of people might be sharing a news item or video. On Twitter it's always possible to see what the biggest trends or hashtags are—will Facebook move toward showing globally popular content, even to a small degree?

Facebook Versus Google

Google has been the 900-pound gorilla of Internet marketing and web traffic for years now, receiving the majority of all search traffic, remaining the top website on the Internet for years. After handily dispatching all its competitors, including Yahoo! and Bing, and purchasing YouTube, which is the second most searched site on the Internet, it seemed no one could challenge them.

However, Facebook has been neck and neck with Google for the past year, and it no longer seems unlikely that Facebook might overtake the search giant. What's more, Facebook's ad revenues continue to climb, and it uses keyword technology in its News Feed to group related posts (see Figure 11.2).

If Facebook improves on its keyword-finding abilities and extends that kind of targeting to its advertising, it will overcome the last barrier to targeting superiority and unlock even greater ROI for advertisers. And this could relegate Google to a disappointing also-ran within two to three years. Google's competitive advantage has always been understanding exactly what people want right now (buying intent signaled by keywords), and Facebook's has been its effectiveness at social media. Google has been unable to crack the social puzzle sufficiently to get big momentum, so if Facebook figures out keyword intent within social activities, Facebook will win.

Figure 11.2   *An example of how Facebook groups posts according to common topics.*

Increasing Ways to Connect

As previously suggested, Facebook has the opportunity to distinguish itself as the single login across the interwebs. Along with this, Facebook could provide tools to these websites that could be integrated easily and also have users interacting with the Facebook platform. An example of this is the Meebo toolbar, used on several sites such as TMZ and Shape. Besides allowing for drag-and-drop sharing of images and videos, the Meebo toolbar allows users to access their instant-messaging services, including Facebook, directly from the website on which the toolbar is integrated. Facebook could move forward with something similar but include tighter integration into Facebook. To do this right, though, Facebook would need to provide tools that would be helpful to the website owners and their community. If it is useful to the website owner, possibly by providing tools that otherwise could be used only by installing multiple plug-ins, Facebook would see a viral effect of the toolbar used.

Skype has continued to increase in popularity with both individuals and the business community as an instant-messaging service and a cheap way to connect with others via video, and also as a substitute for phone service (see Figure 11.3).

Figure 11.3 *Skype and Facebook functionality are merging after Skype was bought by Microsoft, which owns part of Facebook.*

Justin suggested in the second edition that Facebook could chip away at Skype with a video chat service, but in July 2011, Skype and Facebook teamed up to merge functionality. What's interesting is that Microsoft bought Skype, as well as a small percentage of Facebook, and when buying Skype, Microsoft CEO Steve Ballmer insisted on meeting with Mark Zuckerberg to create a functional and a strategic alliance. All of this is part of their war against major competitor Google.

An Endless Rainbow of Options

Over the coming months and years, Facebook can and will implement many more features. Some of these will be refreshes of current features, whereas many others will be new ways for us to become even more obsessed with the social network. The predictions that we have made are only a few of the many that we, our colleagues, and our industry discuss regularly. An entire book could be written about predictions for Facebook's next move.

Whatever these new features are, we encourage you to review them with marketer's eyes. Explore how you can use these features to be more helpful, develop community, and engage your fans, prospects, and customers.

Signing Off

Whether you choose to use Facebook solely as a personal social network to connect with friends and family or use some of the suggestions in this book to help humanize and grow your company, remember that Facebook is a tool. The real value of Facebook is how you use the various features for you and your community.

Facebook is positioned to become the first social network to reach one billion users. With that growth will come more features, more acquisitions, and hopefully, more ways for you and your company to connect with your prospects, customers, colleagues, and fans.

It has been our goal over the course of this book to expose you to the many ways you can use Facebook as part of your company's marketing plan. Not all the features or ideas described will be useful for your company. It is our hope, though, that you have *some* information that will be helpful to you—some information that is actionable and has you eager to finish these last few pages and implement the to-do list you created as you've been reading. The learning doesn't stop here, though.

We also really want to hear your feedback on the book to help improve future editions and, especially, we want to hear whether the content of the book has helped you or your company in any way. Feel free to contact us at any time by dropping a line to brian@briancarteryeah.com.

We know that your time is extremely valuable, and we thank you for spending the time with us you carved out to read the book!

Index

Safari Books Online

FREE
Online Edition

Your purchase of *Facebook® Marketing, Third Edition* includes access to a free online edition for 45 days through the **Safari Books Online** subscription service. Nearly every Que book is available online through **Safari Books Online**, along with thousands of books and videos from publishers such as Addison-Wesley Professional, Cisco Press, Exam Cram, IBM Press, O'Reilly Media, Prentice Hall, and Sams.

Safari Books Online is a digital library providing searchable, on-demand access to thousands of technology, digital media, and professional development books and videos from leading publishers. With one monthly or yearly subscription price, you get unlimited access to learning tools and information on topics including mobile app and software development, tips and tricks on using your favorite gadgets, networking, project management, graphic design, and much more.

Activate your FREE Online Edition at
informit.com/safarifree

STEP 1: Enter the coupon code: FSXKQZG.

STEP 2: New Safari users, complete the brief registration form. Safari subscribers, just log in.

If you have difficulty registering on Safari or accessing the online edition, please e-mail customer-service@safaribooksonline.com